At 112 years of age

In Benares, 1955

LONG PILGRIMAGE

The Life and Teaching of
Sri Govindananda Bharati

known as

THE SHIVAPURI BABA

by

J. G. BENNETT
in collaboration with
THAKUR LAL MANANDHAR

THE RAINBOW BRIDGE

2·86

Hardback edition first published in Great Britain
in 1965 by Hodder and Stoughton Ltd.

Paperback edition first published by Turnstone Books
37 Upper Addison Gardens, London W14, England

Published by The Rainbow Bridge
A Publishing and Distributing Company Ltd.
3548 22nd Street
San Francisco, California 94114

First printing 1975
ISBN 0-914198-05-X

CONTENTS

With the author, Easter 1962

PREFACE

WHEN Dr. Sarvepalli Radhakrishnan, India's beloved President and her most eminent philosopher, visited Nepal in the spring of 1956 for the coronation of King Mahendra, he was expected to go direct to the Royal Guest House which had been specially prepared for him. Instead, he had no sooner alighted from his plane, than he asked to be taken to the retreat of the Shivapuri Baba, then 130 years old. After the usual greetings of civility, the following conversation took place.

S.R. What is your teaching?

S.B. I teach three disciplines—spiritual, moral and physical.

S.R. The whole truth in so few words?

S.B. Yes.

S.R. (Turning to his entourage): The whole Truth in so few words!

S.B. Yes.

Later, the Shivapuri Baba speaking of this visit said: "Then he explained my speech to the others for about fifteen minutes in a most wonderful manner. Such a brilliant explanation I have never heard in my life. I myself envied his power of explanation. He is a soldier of the Vedic literature—rare in the world. He has no destructive nature. He has only constructive nature. Human love he has got. He looks down upon nobody, no hatred for anybody. When he came, he only Namaskaraed me. Before he went, he placed his head upon my feet. Such a thing is most difficult for a man of his position. When I said: I teach three disciplines etc., I saw feelings of shame and horror rise up in his face—shame because for all his scholarship, he had not understood what was at the bottom of life, and horror because after so long living in another belief he feared that he was too old to change his way of life now."

To write a book on the life and teachings of such a man as the Shivapuri Baba, whom I met for the first time when he was already 135 years old, would be an act of unpardonable presumption but

7

for two saving factors. The first is that the Shivapuri Baba himself said that I ought to write about his teachings and saw the account of his life in manuscript before he died in January 1963. The second is that I have been privileged to receive from Mr. Thakur Lal Manandhar, who has been his devotee for nearly thirty years, copies of notes, made over this long period, of talks with the Master. Mr. Manandhar has kindly consented to let his name be joined with mine on the title page of this book.

I must, however, hasten to make it clear that the text remains my responsibility. The Shivapuri Baba told me to set out his teaching so that it would be understood as easily by Europeans as by Indians. That meant a careful adaptation of terminology to avoid excessive use of the technical terms of Hindu philosophy as they occur in the Bhagavad Gita. I submitted the manuscript to Mr. Manandhar, and he kindly made corrections wherever he felt that I was departing seriously from the intention of the Shivapuri Baba. Nevertheless, much must remain as heard through my ears and understood with my, obstinately Western, heart and mind.

The teaching of a man like the Shivapuri Baba does not take the form of a fixed doctrine, the same for all conditions of man and intended to remain for ever unchanged. As he himself points out in one of the talks recorded in this book, the vitality of any teaching depends upon the combination of an unchanging foundation of Truth and a constantly varying superstructure of ideas and methods. The foundation is Right Living, SWADHARMA, which has always been, and always will be, demanded of man, as a condition of his welfare in this life and beyond. The Shivapuri Baba does not leave the notion of Right Living in such general terms as to be applicable to almost any doctrine or code. He connects it specifically with the three disciplines of body, mind and spirit. The basic requirements of the three disciplines are the same for all people, all times and all conditions of life, but their practical application varies from age to age, from nation to nation, from individual to individual, and even for the same individual under different conditions and at different times.

It follows that everyone who has been privileged to receive guidance from a great sage like the Shivapuri Baba will have something different to report. I visited him on two occasions at an interval of one year. The second time he spoke differently, and gave me different advice from the first time. I hope that this means that I had assimilated what he told me on my first visit and was ready for stronger meat.

If the same person hears differently at different times, how much more will this be the case for people of different race and religious formation, such as Mr. Manandhar and myself. The marvel is that we have been able to agree over the essentials, and I am deeply grateful for his understanding sympathy with me in a task that I could not hope to accomplish either to his satisfaction or my own.

For twenty-eight years Thakur Lal Manandhar regularly visited the saint once a week, or more often if he could. He brought his sons to him and educated them under his advice. He gave all these years of devoted service as only a Hindu can give to his Guru*. What could I, a foreign visitor who met the aged saint perhaps a dozen times, expect to make of his teaching? There is only one advantage I can claim: for nearly fifty years, I have been searching for the Truth and have assiduously studied the spirituality of all the great traditions. Therefore, nothing that I heard was strange to me or surprising—except the wonderful simplicity and practicality of his exposition. In a single conversation of half-an-hour, he could tell a visitor all that was necessary for the ordering of life and for the attainment of God-Realization. It does not follow that all was understood. He was always ready to resolve doubts and explain difficulties, but it usually transpired that doubts and difficulties were due to faulty attention on the part of the listener. If we could really hear what he had to say, we should have had no need to trouble him twice.

His words were charged with the immense power of his being. He was a true saint who produced an immediate and uplifting effect on everyone who entered his presence. This effect cannot be conveyed in a book and it would be foolish to try. It has always seemed to me that those who have attempted to convey the feelings

* Though as will appear later the Shivapuri Baba would not accept the role of guru and therefore had no 'disciples'.

9

they experienced in the presence of one of the great Indian saints have usually given the impression of a foolish sentimentality, an exaggerated devotion to the person rather than an understanding of his message. Now that I have met such a saint, I have more sympathy with the writers. I would like myself to be able to summon up the language of a poet to convey the sense of joy, wonder and deep peace that we felt simply on entering his wood, before we even saw him. But this would certainly not be his wish, for he always insisted that his person was nothing and that his message alone was to be conveyed.

During the last years of his life he was living near Kathmandu, the capital of Nepal, in a wood dedicated by the Government to the use of holy men, who were free to establish themselves without liability for taxes or other annoyances.

We flew from Delhi on Easter eve 1961, in a Dakota of the Nepalese Airlines, for the flight over the mountains to Kathmandu. It was our first sight of the Himalayas, strangely remote white pinnacles half hidden by high clouds. The mountains that separate the plains of India from the valley of Nepal are almost impassable; one thin road winds back and forth from col to col. I could well understand the perennial failure of the plainsmen to see the dangers threatening from the North, from the vast expanse of Central Asia where so many invasions have been prepared. It is easy to forget what lies beyond the mountains and to look upon India as a self-contained world. We soon landed in the green valley of the Baghmati river to meet two old friends who had been instrumental in making a connection with the saint.

They told us that the Shivapuri Baba's retreat, at Dhruvasthali, was no more than five minutes from the airport, and suggested that we should pay him a visit before going to our hotel. We were tired and uncomfortable after twenty-four hours' flying, but we did not like to miss the chance of seeing him a day earlier than we had expected.

Five minutes by jeep, passing through a Gurkha cantonment, and then a short walk through an evergreen glade took us to the plain wire gate in a tall fence of wire netting that enclosed his retreat. Hermione rattled the gate, and, getting no reply, shouted our names. After a few minutes a slender boy about twelve years old, wearing a white turban, came up the path smiling broadly, unlocked the padlock and bowed us in. As soon as we stepped into the wood, we all felt the same sense of a presence, strong yet very peaceful. The forest birds were singing in full voice; the Himalayan cuckoo, the Koyeli bird.

The path wound gently through the trees for about a furlong and led into a clearing, in the midst of which stood a single-roomed wooden hut enclosed in new brick walls, built recently, as we learned, to protect the frail old man from the severe Himalayan winter. The earth was smooth, evidently swept clean a few hours before. There were small beds of flowers, inconspicuous but very tidy. The whole place showed the loving care that Indians bestow upon places where there are shrines or temples of special sanctity.

As we turned the corner we saw him leaning forward with an animated look towards us, greeting us with palms pressed together in the usual Indian salutation. The first sight of his face brought a gasp of astonishment. It had an unearthly beauty, with hair and beard of the finest texture streaming out like a halo, and eyes that had a penetrating quality that made one feel that one was standing in the presence of a being from another world.

And yet the Shivapuri Baba was wholly without the demeanour one might expect from a Holy Man. At no time, during our many conversations did he make any suggestion that he was to be venerated or even treated as different from ordinary men. His great age sat on him lightly, and yet one cannot doubt that he was speaking precisely and truthfully when he asserted that he was born in 1826. I have met several truly remarkable men in my life, but none who so evidently belonged to a world different from ours. So far from finding his great age hard to credit, I found myself wondering if he might not be even older than he said—as old as the local inhabitants believed him to be.

The Shivapuri Baba, or Sri Govindananda Bharati as he was known on his pilgrimage round the world, made in the latter part of the last century, is little known in the West, and even in India seems to be less known than some of the great Indian saints who, in the past hundred years, have so deeply impressed the world. Nevertheless, those who knew him regarded him as a very great saint. Shortly after my first visit to him, I went to Calcutta and visited the magnificent new building of the Ramakrishna Mission where I met the Vice-President, Mr. Mukharji, Chief Justice of Bengal. He spoke with reverence and affection of the Shivapuri Baba, referring to him as one of the greatest Indian saints and sages of our day—perhaps the greatest of all.

Books on Yoga for Western readers tend to a proliferation of Sanskrit terms which, for lack of clear interpretation, tend more to confuse than to enlighten the reader. This may not be the fault of the author, for it is characteristic of Asiatic thought to avoid precise fixation of meanings. Moreover, Sanskrit is the oldest language still in course of development. Words that are thousands of years old must have changed again and again in meaning. There has been a gradual transformation of meanings, which for words now used in philosophy shows a recognizable sequence. At first, natural objects, inspired religious acts and words became fixed in ritual formulae. The sacred quality thus acquired by these words led to their adoption to express universal, abstract notions. The conviction that the world is mirrored in man suggested psychological interpretations. Meanwhile, the same words were entering common speech and were given quite ordinary, concrete meanings. Writings that made an extraordinary appeal both to the common people and to the learned such as the Bhagavad Gita fixed, once and for all, certain meanings that were probably generally understood at the time they were composed, but are now obscure. Learned commentators, like Shankarāchārya, with fixed convictions produced interpretations that are far removed from the original simplicity of the texts. One of the great merits of the Shivapuri Baba is to have rescued the earlier meanings and restored the text to a simple statement of what life is all about.

I would have preferred to eliminate all Sanskrit technical terms but as he used them himself so freely, I could not do so without distorting his utterance. One secondary, but not inconsiderable, benefit I have derived from working over his explanations is that I was obliged to revive my knowledge of Sanskrit and make a fresh study of the Bhagavad Gita. This has been a wonderful experience. I have seen more in the Celestial Song than I ever guessed and I can understand why the Shivapuri Baba said that the Gita alone can furnish us with a sufficient guide for all the problems of our lives. To help the reader, I have prepared a glossary of all Sanskrit terms that appear in the text. I have done so by giving the old meanings and the common ones alongside of the special technical sense in which the Shivapuri Baba uses the words. Readers who do not want more than the Sage's message addressed to the Western world can omit Chapter 5 in which I have collected, as far as possible, the material that is of special interest to Hindus.

It has been impossible to achieve the unity of treatment I would have wished, for the reason that the Shivapuri Baba spoke differently according to the formation and understanding of his interlocutor. To Thakur Lal, steeped in the wisdom of the Bhāgavad Gita, he spoke the language of the Gita. To Vittachi, he spoke the language of Subud. To the followers of Gurdjieff he spoke in such a way that several believed him to have been one of Gurdjieff's teachers. To Radhakrishnan, he spoke one sentence and that was all he needed. To me, he said things that integrated and illuminated the myriad ideas and experiences of a life-time. To reduce such a living wealth to logical consistency would be to deprive the reader of the best hope of making contact with one of the great souls of our age.

It is strange that a man of such immense wisdom and spiritual power could have remained relatively little known in a world so much in need of a teaching simple, practical and accessible to men of all faiths or no faith, a teaching that can be followed without the slightest compromise with our own religious convictions and social duties. If this book can bring even a few to the realization that Swadharma, Right Living, can mean the same for a Christian, a Jew or a Moslem or a Buddhist, as it does for a Hindu, then I shall have made a small contribution to the greatest of all tasks of our day: the spiritual re-union of mankind.

To write of such a man is a privilege of which I am unworthy and I can only thank those who have helped me. Mr. Thakur Lal Manandhar is more than a helper, and I am indebted to him and

13

his son, Manandhar, for most of the photographs. Mrs. Marjorie von Harter has kindly allowed me to use a photograph she took in 1962. I must also thank those friends who, by relieving me of part of the financial burden, made my two visits to Nepal possible.

CHAPTER ONE

THE QUEST

In the Year of Grace 1826, George the Fourth was King of England. A seven year old girl, living obscurely in Kensington Palace, was eleven years later to become Queen Victoria. George Canning had, for some four years, as Foreign Secretary, been working to convert his country from the role of defender of the ancient privileges to that of champion of the new liberties.

The conquest of India had just been completed by the Mahratta and Burmese wars, and the sub-continent was, for the first time since Aurungzeb, united under *rulers* of an alien race. Fortunately, the British did not reproduce the merciless intolerance of the last Great Mogul. In the same year, 1826, a very great Indian, Ram Mohan Roy, was successful in securing the support of the British Raj for reforms that were, within less than one and a half centuries, to produce Modern India. He was already, in that year, planning the Brahmo Samaj, a spiritual movement which sought to unite Hinduism and Christianity.

Outwardly the world was at peace and full of hope for the future. But there was everywhere a current of unease. Prophecies of the early end of the Age found ready hearers in many parts of the world. In India, at least, the traditional beliefs and customs were well-established. The Varnāshram, or regulation of life by castes and stages, was, especially in Southern India, so firmly entrenched that even a reformer as bold as Ram Mohan Roy made no attempt to fight it.

Such was the world, and such was India, when in 1826, a Brahmin family in the State of Kerala was awakened to rejoice in the birth of twin children, a boy and a girl. The family belonged to the clan or sub-caste of the Nambudris of the highest and purest Brahmin descent. The grandfather, Achyutam, was known far and wide as a great astrologer, to whom Brahmins and Princes resorted for advice upon the vital problems on which Indians to this day seek guidance from the planets. A family profoundly religious, rooted in tradition, and little touched by the upheavals that were but recently rife in North and Central India.

When the baby boy was born, he smiled, even as he drew his first breath. He was brought to his grandfather, who announced that the signs of his birth and the smile signified that a great sannyasin had come into the world, and that his family line would come to an end, as it had fulfilled its purpose on earth.

The early part of his life followed the usual course. At five, he entered upon the Ashram or stage of studentship—Brahmacharya —and by the time he was twelve he had mastered the four principal Vedas and the two subsidiary works, the Dhanurveda and the Ayurveda. His grandfather was his guru, and he completed his student period by about 1840. Achyutam had meanwhile entered the third phase of his life—that of the Vānaprastha, or hermit, and decided to retire to the forest far from his home.

At the age of eighteen, that is, in 1844, the young Brahmin decided to abandon the world. He made a will entitling his twin sister to inherit their paternal property and followed his grand-father to the forest. The future Edward VII was a three-year-old baby in Buckingham Palace. The greatest Indian saint of the nine-teenth century, Ramakrishna, was ten years old, and was about to enter the first of his great spiritual ecstacies. The young Brahmin was leaving a world already troubled, though few could have fore-seen the upheavals of the next ten years.

Soon after he joined his grandfather in the forest, on the banks of the Narbada river in the upper Deccan, he began to prepare him-self for his vocation as a sannyasin. In the Vedic religion, as codified in the great Law Books of Manu, Gautama and Vasishtha, two ways of perfection are laid open to man. One is the way of the four Ashramas or stages of life. This consists in the fulfilment of the duties of a householder, the begetting and training of sons to follow him, the establishment of a family, and the performance of all the elaborate ritual that is incumbent upon the priestly caste of Brahmins. These duties require some forty-two years for their accomplishment. At the age of sixty-three, the Grand Climateric, the Brahmin householder has seen his sons grow to man's estate, his daughters' families established, and his religious duties transferred to his eldest son and heir. He is then a free man. He may then retire to the forest or other solitary place, accompanied by his wife, if she is still alive. This third stage of life enables him to prepare himself for the abandonment of all earthly ties. When he feels himself ready, he enters the fourth estate, that of Sannyasin, and either remains in the forest or wanders from village to village, supported by the alms joyfully offered wherever he goes.

Such is the normal life. To those who discover in themselves a sufficiently firm resolution to abandon everything from the start, a second way is open. They can cut out the periods as householder and forest dweller, and enter directly upon the final stage of abandonment of the world.

For this way also, rules have long been established in India. They are mainly due to the great reformer Shankarāchārya, who lived from A.D. 780 to 820, and founded twelve orders of Sannyasins in all parts of India. At the present time, there are four main divisions, each with its own monastery headed by a spiritual leader bearing the name of the founder Shankarāchārya. Each of the orders bears a name shared by all Sannyasins belonging to it. Ramakrishna was initiated in the East by Tota Puri, and all monks of his order bear the name of Puri. The northern Sannyasins are Saraswatis and the western, Giri.

The future Shivapuri Baba waited for the death of his grandfather before taking his final vows. When preparing for death, his grandfather told him that he had set aside a large sum in the form of diamonds and other precious stones which he was to guard until he had attained Jiwanmukti or God-Realization. Then, in accordance with the tradition established by the example of Shankarāchārya himself, he would have to make a pilgrimage round the world. This had always been interpreted to mean a pilgrimage on foot to the four corners of India, visiting all the holy places and returning to his birthplace. In his case, the pilgrimage round the world, said his grandfather, was to be taken literally, and for this reason he had prepared a large sum of money to enable him to travel freely in countries where wandering sannyasins were not yet known.

When he had buried his grandfather and completed all obligatory duties on his behalf, the young man set out to visit the Shānkaramutt of the South and receive his initiation as a Sannyasin. He took the name of Govindānanda Bhārati. Speaking of this, he said that this initiation was not necessary for him, as he knew what he had to do, but he accepted it as an act of piety.

He then set out into the jungle that stretched at that time for hundreds of miles along the banks of the Narbada river. In the final stages of the journey, he did not meet another human being for fourteen days. The place he finally selected was in the depth of the Narbada Forest protected from chance visitors by deep impenetrable jungle. There he could find the self-grown food he needed to maintain life—the only external obligation that remains to the Sannyasin during his period of complete seclusion.

The path that Govindānanda intended to follow was that of Itambhara Prajna or Absolute Realization of God beyond all forms and images. This is reached by stages which are recognizably similar to those followed by the great contemplatives. No one can start from the end, that is, from the contemplation of God as Absolute Will beyond Being itself. To reach Itambhara Prajna there must be a progressive elimination of all that can support and comfort the mind. Only when all is stripped away, and the soul enters the absolute nakedness that is beyond consciousness and beyond understanding, can it make that final act of the Pure Will whereby all distinctions disappear and the Individual and the Absolute are made one.

On the way to the Absolute there are stages of relative perfection, each accompanied by its own mode of God-Realization. As each is attained, it is to be rejected as soon as it becomes apparent that any separation still remains.

How many times did the future saint encounter God, only to plunge more deeply into the unknowable Abyss? Year after year passed. Govindānanda tells us that he soon lost count of time. In the Indian jungle the years can pass with no outward signs but the dry and wet seasons, and even the Monsoon rains pass unnoticed by the Sannyasin who has withdrawn his attention from the natural order. It is easy to write that he spent more than twenty years in total solitude, except for the wild animals who had become his friends and only companions. It is not at all easy for those of us Europeans who have perhaps longed to be alone for a time, but never achieved even a month's complete solitude, to picture to ourselves the effect upon a sensitive soul of such a life—passed during the years of greatest natural vigour between twenty-five and forty-eight years of age. To live only upon roots, fruits and wild grains may be very healthy, and no doubt one would soon get used to it. To remain alone for a quarter of a century without exchanging a word with another human being must indeed call for a strong, pure mind, if it is to be borne without loss of sanity. It seems to me that the hardest part must be to spend year after year without any certainty as to when, or even whether, the final enlightenment, the Beatific Vision, would be granted. Most of us can bear constraints for a time; it is when we have no assurance of relief that our courage is tried beyond endurance.

The Shivapuri Baba was emphatic in his talks with us that withdrawal from the world need not mean denial of the world, or its rejection. For him it meant the elimination of all actions that were not required for the maintenance of life. It is precisely these actions that unite us to Nature, that is Prakriti, and establish in the perfected man the same relationship to his own body as the Supreme Brahman has to the Universal Prakriti. This is a relationship of mutual love, and there can be no doubt that the love of nature filled Govindānanda then, as it filled the Shivapuri Baba as he sat in his forest retreat to receive us a hundred years later.

The years went by. The inner life deepened, and strengthened. We cannot know what spiritual crises were surmounted, for so far as I am aware he has never spoken of his years of solitary meditation. Meanwhile, the outer world went on its way. The Indian Mutiny (1856) came and passed unnoticed. In 1961, he told an Indian journalist that he knew nothing of it until many years later.

India was passing through one of the greatest transformations of history, casting off, almost unperceived to herself and the world, the traditions that neither great reformers, such as the founders of the Buddhist and Jain religions, nor great conquerors, from Alexander the Great to Akbar, had been able to destroy: the traditions of the Vedic society, inherited from a past so remote that they still retain unmistakable traces of the last Ice Age that ended more than ten thousand years ago. India, for the first time in three millenia, was looking beyond her own boundaries for the instruments with which to fashion a new life. The repudiation of British rule had not yet become general. Great Indians like Surendranath Banerjea and G. K. Gokhale were opening the doors of India to western learning, western culture and even western ways of life. Before long, fiery souls like B. G. Tilak and Aurobindo Ghose were to combine assimilation of western instruments with the uncompromising assertion of India's spiritual independence. From this to the demand for political independence was a step that was bound to come.

But all these events, and those in the world at large, were non-existent for the solitary recluse sitting in his jungle retreat and waiting for God, like the boy in the story he was to tell so often.

At last came the supreme moment. As he has so often said, it came 'in a flash'. God was seen and all problems were solved! Since the whole of this book will be concerned with the consequences of this moment, I should have gladly elaborated upon the simple statement. But who could ever describe in words what it means to 'see' God as Absolute, beyond all forms and all manifestations? Hundreds of mystics have attempted the task, many of them without having attained to the authentic and final Vision. Before those who have had the vision, we can only close our eyes with holy dread. Their very look tells us that they have drunk the milk of paradise, and that there is nothing more to be attained. Of all human beings I have met in my life, none has produced upon me more convincingly that impression of one who has attained the utmost limit of perfection possible for a man.

What remained to be done? He was then fifty years old and there were still duties to be fulfilled. There was the promise to his grandfather to make a pilgrimage that would englobe the earth. There were religious obligations incumbent upon the sannyasin who has attained God-Realization.

The strangest moment must be that of re-emergence into the world. Monks and nuns long cloistered have described the sense of unreality with which they encounter the world that men call 'real'. How much more must this be true of the solitary ascetic who has spent ten, twenty, thirty years in solitude, whose food has been roots, fruits and wild grains, whose mind has grown pure and strong in contemplation of the Absolute Reality, and who has not been supported by the practice of the religious observances which are shared even in the strictest of contemplative orders. There must always be the danger for a Sannyasin who goes into complete solitude, that his way of life will become a fixed habit. He can grow to be contented with his diet and the company of his animal friends, and forgetting rather than abandoning the world, becomes so absorbed into his environment that he will end by becoming an enlightened and blissful animal of the forest. To resist assimilation, the yearning for self-realization must burn with undiminished fire, and this must produce a state of tension almost beyond the power of man to endure.

Such were the musings, aroused in my mind as I sat and gazed at the old old man who had been through it all, and who had returned to the world, full of vigour and with a lively interest in all human affairs.

He told us nothing of his life as a recluse and far too little of his subsequent wanderings. The account I shall give has been pieced together from random scraps of information, and it may be that some of the most interesting events have been lost for ever. He cared so little for his life, that even when he was encouraging me to write this book, he would not answer more than a tithe of my questions as to where he had been and whom he had met.

From the forest, he made his way westward to Baroda where Sayaji Rao III had just been placed on the throne under the tutelage of my late father-in-law H. A. Elliot, who, although a cousin of Lord Minto, was later to come in conflict with the Viceroy for his championship of B. G. Tilak. The Shivapuri Baba remembered these events and told me that he had 'taught Tilak some astronomy'. This interested me greatly because I regard Tilak's *Arctic Home in the Vedas* as one of the most remarkable reconstructions of ancient history ever made. It could not have been accomplished without a very unusual spiritual insight.

The pilgrimage, always on foot, included all the holy places of India. In Calcutta, he visited Ramakrishna, eight years younger than himself, and already known and loved throughout India.

In Baroda, he met Aurobindo Ghose, one of the great interpreters of Indian spirituality both to India herself and to the West. Aurobindo was in service of the Galkwad of Baroda at the time, and his talk with the saint, radiant with the light of God-Realization, must have made a profound impression upon one who was to make, in middle life, the tremendous decision to abandon a public career at the moment of highest achievement, to become in his turn a sannyasin and, eventually, a saint. Aurobindo knew him as Lalu and seems to have spoken of him to his disciples in his later years. The memory of the encounter was a decisive factor in the direction taken by him in later life. Readers of this book who are familiar with Aurobindo's writings will recognize the similarity of outlook, especially in the obligation to combine the search for God with the fulfilment of the duties of the external life.

The pilgrimage round the world was now to start in earnest. It was no more formal duty. There was a real task to be accomplished. The sannyasin who had met God face-to-face, was required also to know man in all his ways. The study of mankind was an undertaking that was to require an even longer period than that devoted to waiting for God.

After India, Afghanistan. He said this several times. In one sense it was natural and inevitable, for a westerly pilgrimage on foot must lead out of India by the Khyber Pass. It seems that he had met the first Agha Khan, Hasan Ali Shah, and was well acquainted with the Ismaili tradition. The very great influence of the Agha Khan may have been responsible for the opening to him of doors in the Islamic world which would usually be closed to a Hindu. He told us that he spent some time in Afghanistan which was, and still is, one of the chief centres of the spiritual life of Islam.

From there, he went to Persia. The Shah, Nasreddin, who was related by marriage to the Agha Khan, was in serious trouble with Russia and Britain over the struggle against Aghan independence. All we know is that he received the Indian saint, who was helped on his way westward.

His next objective was Mecca. Strange as it may seem, he told us that he had been to the Holy City. This could have been possible only if his journey were sponsored by Muslims of the highest authority, who would vouch for his sanctity. He could no doubt pronounce, without insincerity, the necessary formula "God is One, He alone is to be obeyed, and Muhammad is his servant and his prophet", but this alone was not enough even in those more careless days of Turkish rule to secure entry to the Holy City. To those who understand the true meaning of Islam it is the inward act that makes the true Muslim. Every man, of whatever outward creed is a Muslim, in the true sense of the word, if he is wholly submitted and surrendered to God. This was true of Govindānanda from his childhood. He was, no doubt, recognized by a Sufi Brotherhood whose guarantee of orthodoxy would be accepted in Mecca.

I may say here that his understanding of Islam was so complete, that when I first met him I took for granted that he was a Muslim, and even said so in an article I wrote about him at the time. There is a special way of speaking about God that seems to characterize the true Muslim. It combines the sense of God as transcending the creation with that of His intimate presence within the human soul. It was just in this way that the Shivapuri Baba spoke. Later, I came to understand that he spoke from a direct experience of the mystery of the Divine Totality—transcendent, immanent, personal and yet Absolute. This enabled him to express the truth of all religions in such a way as to make the listener feel that he was a Hindu, a Buddhist, a Muslim, or a Christian, and each of them completely—without reservation.

I do not mean by this that he was prepared to identify himself with any religious faith. His criticism of each of the principal expressions of the ancient Vedic religion which are current today will appear later in this book. His attitude to Islam was summed up in a few words: "The pilgrims at Mecca are inspired with true religious fervour, but I did not find myself attracted to Islam as it is today."

23

From Mecca to the Holy Land, to Jerusalem, the home of Christianity, is a journey of 800 miles, largely through semi-desert. I cannot but pause to comment on the incredible feat represented by a pilgrimage round the world on foot. He told me, and I see no reason to doubt his word, that he had covered eighty per cent of the land journey on foot. It took him forty years, from 1875 to 1915 to circumambulate this planet. The journey is more than the 25,000 miles round the equator, for he followed a zig-zag path far to the north and far to the south of the equator. To appreciate it one must know something of the countries he traversed. I have more than once flown in daytime the long journey from India to Europe. Persia alone is nearly 1,000 miles across. To go by the northerly route is the only practical way, and this means crossing mountain ranges and valleys over and over again, for a distance greater than from London to Rome.

It is possible most of the way to choose friendly valleys with villages not too far apart, where a saintly pilgrim can be assured of hospitality. But when it comes to the pilgrimage to Mecca, it is an altogether different story. I know something of the Arabian desert and how daunting it is even on a camel. I have met one other man, also a saint, Farhad Dede of Aleppo, who made the pilgrimage from Aleppo to Mecca on foot when he was nearly seventy years old. He took six months to make the pilgrimage and intended to walk back, but was prevailed upon to accept a passage by sea offered to him by a pious pilgrim from Turkey. I could tell from the way that those who knew Farhad Dede spoke of his endurance, that the journey was regarded as an exceptional feat for an old man. The Shivapuri Baba must have been nearly as old—but this was only a small part of his entire pilgrimage—not more than a thirtieth part of the whole journey round the world.

At some date early in the 1890's, he arrived in Jerusalem and spent some time there. Thence to Istanbul. I have made this part of the journey more than once, and can picture the endless miles of the Anatolian Steppe and the stolidity of the Turkish peasantry of Asia Minor, so unlike the Indians or Russians and yet so religious and so hospitable.

In most of the countries he visited he was presented to the

reigning sovereign: but not to Abdul Hamid II, Sultan of Turkey, that strange, suspicious, unreliable and yet much misunderstood man. I know that from Turkey he went almost immediately through the Balkans into Greece, and from Athens to Rome—probably by sea.

He told me that he had spent some time in Rome in order to come to understand better the Christian Religion. From his talks with me I could see that he had more than a theoretical knowledge of Catholicism. I was astonished to see how well he understood the place that the Blessed Virgin Mary occupies in the hearts and minds of Catholics. I shall return to the talks he had with me on the subject because they concern me personally more than his life story and journey round the world.

Unfortunately, I omitted to ask what he had found, and what form his meetings had taken or whom he had met in the Vatican. In those days Rome was still far from having reached its present position of openness to all who, under whatever form, believe in and worship God.

Italy did not retain him long. He visited most of the countries of Europe. He spoke of meeting the Kaiser Wilhelm II, and Queen Emma of the Netherlands. This I recently learned independently from friends in Holland. He certainly met many other interesting people but would not tell us about them or his reasons for meeting them.

Then, in 1896, he was invited to England. Apparently the invitation came from Queen Victoria's Indian Secretariat, then dominated by that extraordinary man the Munshi Abdul Karim. Govindānanda Bharati, who was known in England as Govinda, spent four years in England from 1896 to 1901. During this time, he visited the Queen eighteen times—'at various castles' as he put it. He told us that his visits were very personal. They were no doubt scrupulously entered in the Queen's diary, and, equally scrupulously, cut out by Princess Beatrice when she carried out, only too well, the task of editing them and 'removing all that could hurt anyone's feelings'.

His stay in England was a prolonged interruption of his pilgrimage. He travelled all over the country, sometimes invited to great country houses but also wandering on foot from village to village. He was able to recognize and remember my description of the Welsh hills, and spoke of Snowdon and his visit to someone who lived within sight of it. He also visited the Isle of Man, where he stayed with the Wilkinson family, whose young son, then introduced to him, was to play a part in his life some twenty-five years later.

His excellent English, enlivened with apt stories from the Mahābhārata or Ramayana, or even, I suspect, sometimes invented by himself, his quick wit, and his profound wisdom; and no doubt, most of all, the irresistible attraction that the power of sanctity exerts upon even half-receptive people—combined to make him sought after by the hostesses of the end of the century. He went everywhere and met everyone freely. He spoke of Lord Salisbury and Lord Randolph Churchill who, no doubt, had much to ask him about India. He told us of his encounter in 1898 with George Bernard Shaw who professed contempt for Yogis and their like, saying to Govindānanda: "You Indian saints are the most useless of men; you have no respect for time." His reply was: "It is you who are slaves of time. I live in Eternity".

I wish it were possible to say something of his eighteen private visits to Queen Victoria. Her Indian entourage was mainly composed of Muslims under the stern eye of the Munshi Abdul Karim. So far as I know Govindānanda was the first Sannyasin to meet the Queen. He was not, of course, the first Indian of high spiritual development to come to England. A few years earlier Vivekananda, the closest disciple of Ramakrishna and founder of the Rāmakrishna mission, had passed through England on his way to the Congress of Religions in Chicago (1893), where he delivered his inspired address on the Unity of All Faiths. But Vivekananda did not stay long in England nor did his work receive the official encouragement it deserved. Govindānanda came without mission or purpose; but, for some reason unknown to me, his arrival was expected by the Queen. In his many contacts during his stay in England, he must have done more than any other single man of his time to awaken the realization that Indian Spirituality had a gift of immense value to offer to the world.

26

At that time the Queen was deeply interested in the spiritual life of the Indian people whom she loved so tenderly. As her diary shows, she was immensely conscious of the responsibility that her country had assumed towards India, and sincerely entertained the same feelings of loving concern towards her Indians as towards her own people. Unfortunately, her feminine instincts were not understood by her own Ministers. She, almost alone, realized that the only durable bonds between England and India were those of love and mutual respect. Most Englishmen were still obsessed with ideas of Empire and, worse, self-interest.

Beyond all else, the Queen had been concerned, since the death of the Prince Consort, with the mystery of death. However she might turn towards her outward duties, the mystery never left her. In Govindānanda she met a man who had seen for himself what is beyond the veil of death. I cannot doubt that her great hope was that he should enable her to see for herself. Her insistence that he should not leave England during her lifetime is evidence that his help must have been very real.

After the Queen's death in 1901, he resumed his pilgrimage, crossing the Atlantic and arriving in America, where he was already expected and sought after. Arriving soon after the assassination of McKinley, he met Theodore Roosevelt, then beginning his remarkable term as President. He spent two or three years in the U.S.A. Vivekananda had inaugurated the Vedanta movement and returned to India, to die at the early age of 39. Many invitations were pressed upon Govindānanda to stay in the U.S.A. and inspire and help those seeking to understand Indian spirituality. When we asked about this he said: "A man like Vivekananda was chosen by God to help the world. That was his Dharma which he had to fulfil. Like Shankara he died young; but he had fulfilled his Dharma. I have no such task in the world; therefore I was free to go my own way."

Leaving the U.S.A. about 1904, he made his way southward, always on foot, to reach Mexico where he met the already ageing dictator, Porfirio Diaz, whose friendship with Theodore Roosevelt had brought peace to central America after generations of conflict. But Mexico then, as seen by the pilgrim walking from village to village, was a miserable country where millions of Indians were living in virtual slavery.

On and on southward he journeyed to reach the Andes, the western counterpart of the Himalayas, under whose shadow he was to pass his latter years, southward through Colombia and Peru and up to the high passes. I do not know that country, but two ladies who visited him with me and knew it well could confirm the accuracy of his memory. He described the route he had followed and how, through losing his way, he had come, by an unexplored route, to Lake Titicaca, the highest great lake in the world. The water is 12,500 feet above sea level, and along its 110 miles length are the remains of one of the greatest of the lost civilizations of the world. At the time of his visit Titicaca was almost unknown to the rest of the world, and I could not but wonder at the insight which made Govindānanda seek it out to find a contact with one of the sources of human culture.

After a considerable stay in South America, he took ship for the Pacific Islands, passing through New Zealand and Australia, and coming to Japan in 1913. The outbreak of the first World War found him in Sinkiang. He followed the ancient pilgrim's way into Nepal, discovering—as he told us—that the ascent of Mount Everest should be made by that route finally taken by John Hunt and his party in 1952.

He came to Benares, where he stayed with Pandit Madan Mohan Malaviya. He donated Rs 50,000 to the fund which the Pandit was collecting for founding the Benares Hindu University. He was even offered the Chancellorship, but he had to reject this offer being a Sannyasin.

Before he could regard his pilgrimage as accomplished, one last duty remained: to return to his home as a wandering mendicant. When he reached Kerala—after nearly seventy years—all was so changed that he could not find his own home. When he had taken his vows of poverty as a Sannyasin, he had made a will leaving the paternal property to his twin-sister. They had no other brothers and sisters, so when she also decided to leave the world, she had sold everything and distributed the proceeds to the poor. No trace of his sister or his home remained. The prediction of his grandfather that his family would end with him had been fulfilled. Some of the money prepared by his grandfather still remained, so he returned to the Narbada Forest and buried it with the rest of the treasure.

All was at last accomplished, and he decided to go to Nepal to live in the forest, without, this time, cutting himself off from human contacts. Here an unexpected difficulty awaited him. According to the regulations then obtaining in Nepal, pilgrims from India were not permitted to stay for more than one week after the Holy Day of Shivaratri. Most of the pilgrims are Sadhus who come up from India through the passes, though many pious householders undertake the arduous journey to the Festival which occurs in the month of March each year.

When he was notified that he would be required to return to India, he consented; but, on his way to the police headquarters, a carriage was passing and an Englishman leaned out and called to him, "Are you not Govinda?" It was the same Mr. Wilkinson who, while still a schoolboy, he had met twenty years earlier in the Isle of Man. I can well understand that he could not fail to recognize him. Even at the age of 100, he continued to have the same upright carriage, the same splendid black hair and above all the same wonderful eyes as at the time of his God-Realization fifty years earlier.

Wilkinson had meanwhile become British Resident in Nepal and a close friend of the Ruler. He was able to secure exceptional treatment for his friend, who was thus able to make his home in the Shivapuri Peak, not far from Kathmandu the capital of Nepal.

The name of Govindānanda Bharati was left behind, as he had left behind eighty years earlier the Brahminical name and the name of his family. He was, for the Nepalese, a saintly old man living in the Shivapuri Forest—the Shivapuri Baba. By this name he was to be known for the thirty-eight years of life remaining to be accomplished.

Mr. Wilkinson used to go regularly, every Sunday, to visit the forest retreat, where he performed the duties of a disciple, sweeping the earth, preparing a meal and waiting in silence until the hour for conversation arrived. In the evening he would return to the capital and resume his duties as a high official of the British Raj. This continued until Wilkinson retired and returned home to England, where he died in 1939.

According to the Shivapuri Baba, Wilkinson was one of those rare men who could combine an active life with that complete devotion to the search for the prajnā consciousness which brings man to the knowledge of God and of the meaning of life.

By this time, the Shivapuri Baba had passed his century, and his reputation was spreading from Nepal to India, and even to the Buddhist countries of Burma and Ceylon. He firmly rejected every attempt to make his forest retreat a centre of pilgrimage—an ashram—with the attendant community of ardent seekers for help on the path to enlightenment, the married disciples with their families and the restless crowd of visitors, sight-seers and tourists. He told us that he had made it plain to all that if any such attempt were made, he would disappear to a place where no one could track him down.

I confess that this rejection of the traditional role of a Mahatma, or Great Teacher, had attracted me even before I met the Shivapuri Baba in person. When I did at last meet him, I could see for myself that he was in the full sense of the word a free man—completely indifferent to praise or blame, one who knew what and who he was, and what he had to do during his remaining years of life, and why.

It seems to me, though he never said so or even hinted at such a possibility, that his outward task in this life was to guide and help those who occupied positions of responsibility. He himself regarded the 'outward' duty as an obligation, the performance of which cannot bring salvation, but is nevertheless an obligation that cannot be shirked. He certainly did not have any of the snobbery that afflicts too many Holy Men, of delighting in having spoken with the great of this world. When he authorized the writing of this book, I asked him to tell me about some of the interesting people he had met. He refused to help me, saying: "That has no importance. You should write about my teaching, not about me."

Some thirty years before he died, the Shivapuri Baba discovered that he had contracted cancer of the gums. Deciding to try orthodox medical treatment, he removed from the forest to a place near to Kathmandu. At first, he built a small hut in Kirātesh-war, which is close to the present site, and stayed there till 1943. He allowed himself to be examined by doctors brought by his devotees, but seeing that no medical treatment would help, he followed a procedure known to Yogis, and the cancer lost its virulence and died away. Since that time, he began to smoke cigarettes. I was informed by Mr. Manandhar that he was ex-amined a year or two before his death by two American doctors, who confirmed that he had traces of jaw cancer that had cleared up, and that there was no sign of any return of the condition. When the disease was cured, he moved to the present site locally known as Dhruvasthali. This is a forest that lies behind the temple of Pashupati Nath, where Sadhus can stay if they like without having to pay anything to the authorities. He built him-self a small wooden hut. More recently this was enclosed in brick walls to protect him from the winter cold.

During his thirty-eight years in Nepal, he must have been visited by thousands of Sadhus, householders and foreigners who were fortunate enough to hear of him. My first knowledge of his existence came in 1933 from Professor Ratnasuriya, a learned Buddhist from Ceylon, who was also a great authority on Sanskrit Epigraphy. In 1930, or thereabouts, Ratnasuriya, though a sincere Buddhist, became dissatisfied with religion as it was practised by the Bhikhus or Buddhist monks of Ceylon. He had sought advice from an aged monk, then living in a forest retreat, and who was reputed to have attained enlightenment, that elusive goal of the Noble Eightfold Path. The Bhikhu professed himself unable to give advice to a worldly man, and advised Ratnasuriya to under-take a pilgrimage to India, and make a point of visiting an aged Swami who was then living in solitude in the foothills of the Himalayas in Nepal. This was the Shivapuri Baba.

Ratnasuriya told me some years later the story of his journey, which, if I remember rightly, took place in 1930. He managed to get nominated as the delegate for Ceylon to a religious congress in Northern India, and so was able to visit Nepal for a few days. He

31

found his way to the Shivapuri Baba's retreat, thanks to a letter of introduction from the aged Bhikhu. He was told that the Shivapuri Baba was more than a hundred years old, and refused to permit anyone to live near his retreat, threatening if his peace was disturbed, to disappear into the inaccessible regions that lie between Tibet and Bhutan. Ratnasuriya found a man with black hair who, though small of stature and slight of build, had a splendid physique and showed a lively interest in all that Ratnasuriya could tell him of Ceylon, which he apparently had visited some fifty years earlier. He answered Ratnasuriya's question by saying that he should go to London, where he would find the spiritual teaching that corresponded to his own nature. This had astonished Ratnasuriya, who had, like many Asiatics, looked upon England and all European countries as sunk in materialism and remote from the sources of true spirituality. The Shivapuri Baba assured him that he was mistaken and that, on the contrary, he would find in England something that had been almost entirely lost in Ceylon. Moreover, he assured Ratnasuriya that he would find the move to England as easy as his visit to Nepal.

One striking memory of his visit was the sudden arrival from the depths of the forest of a full-grown leopard, which entered as a domestic cat might have done to sit beside the Shivapuri Baba. Ratnasuriya had been unable to master a moment of terror, but the Shivapuri Baba explained that those who live for many years in complete solitude in the forest—as he had done earlier in his life—become so friendly with wild animals that no fear is felt on either side.

When Ratnasuriya returned to Ceylon, he found an invitation to apply for a post as lecturer in Sanskrit Epigraphy at the School of Oriental Studies in London. Feeling sure that this had been foretold by the Shivapuri Baba, he accepted, although the post meant a certain loss of status. Soon after settling in London, Ratnasuriya was brought into contact with Ouspensky, and was immediately convinced that Gurdjieff's teaching and method would satisfy his spiritual needs. He did in fact remain a follower of Gurdjieff's teaching for the rest of his life. In 1949 I took him to Paris to meet Gurdjieff, with whom he spoke for little more than two minutes. Nevertheless, to the end of his life, two years later, he spoke of this meeting as the culmination of his search for Reality.

Ratnasuriya told us something of the teaching of the Shivapuri Baba which, he said, appeared to him much nearer to Gurdjieff's system than to orthodox Hinduism. He had intended to revisit the Shivapuri Baba, but war and the aftermath of war prevented him.

Knowing Ratnasuriya to be an experienced and critical student, I was impressed by his assertion that the Shivapuri Baba was the only true saint whom he had met on his fairly extensive travels in India, Ceylon and Burma. I think that the picture of the old man with a wild leopard for his best friend, was more appealing to me than that of the famous Indian spiritual leaders with their ashrams and thousands of adoring followers.

Nevertheless, it did not seem likely that I would ever see the old man. If he was more than a hundred years old in 1930, he was hardly likely to be alive in 1950.

Then, quite unexpectedly, I received in 1955, a visit from a fellow-student of Ouspensky, Mr. H. R., who was connected with one of the great International Institutions set up after the war. His work had taken him to India and he had taken the opportunity to visit Nepal. There he had met the Shivapuri Baba and kindly gave me a copy of the relevant part of his travel diary from which I have taken the following extracts.

"I walked down to Pashupati Nath, where the Aghori Baba lives, in order to visit the Shivapuri Baba, who lives in the jungle on the opposite bank of the river. We went off accompanied by a couple of small boys who came along, I guess, just to see what would happen. We walked about a mile along a track through the forest, climbing several hundred feet above the river, and finally reached a permanent army camp. Passing through this, we found ourselves on the edge of the airfield, which we skirted for some distance and then took a path leading to the left, round the other side of the army camp, and shortly afterwards turned left again along a smaller path into the jungle. A hundred yards and we came to an enclosure (I could not tell how large) surrounded with barbed wire strung from tree to tree, with an occasional post, in which was set a doorway, padlocked on the inside. My guide called out something and shortly afterwards a young man came to the gate, and after a short conversation with my guide, went away in the direction from which he had come, where I could make out through the trees the roof of some small house made out of woven bamboo.

"After a few minutes he came back, smiled at me, and let us in. We followed him along, and saw about thirty or forty feet from the hut I had seen from the gate (where the young man evidently lived) a rather larger hut, very simple, made of bamboo in the shape of a rectangle, and surrounded on all sides by a porch which was screened by chicken wire. At the far end of this house was a figure in white. We walked round the house, and found the Baba standing there. White hair and beard, very clear brown eyes, with smiling-wrinkles at their corners. A smooth forehead, and certainly not in general the appearance of an old man. Quite erect, moving easily. And yet he is said to be 125 years old. He is the same man Ratnasuriya went into the forest to see, and apparently his tame leopard was quite well known. It has died now.

"He smiled, and at once I had the same kind of feeling which I had with Father Nikon from Athos: this was a man who radiated goodness and love. He motioned me through a door-way in the screened porch, inside which was a wooden bench, a wooden chair, and a wide wooden seat which was hung from the roof and supplied with a long tape attached to its back and running through pulleys, so that by sitting in the seat and pulling the other end, you could make it swing back and forth. The place was spotlessly clean, the floor being covered by small grey pebbles. He motioned me to take the chair, and himself, slipping his feet out of his wooden sandals, sat down in the swing, taking with ease and apparent comfort a sitting position which for any ordinary person would have been quite impossible.

"I began by saying I had heard of him through Ratnasuriya. He remembered him, and spoke about him as a very good man. His voice was sweet, not very loud. He spoke with few questions, and his English was more or less perfect. He told me he had spent three years in England and seven years in America. I learned from someone else afterwards that he had been a very learned man, a professor or something, before he left the world.

"I was with him in all for about an hour, and came away in a very emotional state. Here was a man, I felt, who could and did put into practice, in his life, what the System teaches. As we parted, after he had kindly let me take his picture (and he did not dress up, but just slipped his feet into his sandals and stepped outside), he said with this radiant goodness and love quietly: 'Just a little practice of a very simple things.' He was dressed, incidentally, in a very simple sleeveless long garment of thin cotton, under which he wore a string round his waist, which held up a white cloth passing through the crotch."

I myself finally went to visit him, at Easter 1961, and again the following year. I was to be ever thankful that I made the journey; the following notes of my impressions may convey a little of his wonderful quality.

"He is a very, very old man. He suffers from bronchitis in the winter and from asthma at all times. He can only walk a few paces in the day. Although very feeble in body, he is wonderfully alert in mind. He can see and hear as well as a man a hundred years younger. He still has his own teeth, and a fine head of hair and beard. His memory is phenomenal. He seems to be able to recall all the places he has visited and to see them again in his mind's eye. When questions are put to him, he listens intently and scarcely gives the questioner time to finish before answering with animated voice and gesture. One does not at all have the feeling of being before someone who is old and feeble. He can speak for two hours, and at the end his audience is more tired than himself. His quick graceful movements and gay laughter give the impression of youth. And yet, with it all, one can never forget that he can see beyond the veil of consciousness. His immense experience of life and his understanding of human nature are there, but they are merely instruments. He himself remains impassive behind the brilliant eyes that see everything and the mind that understands us all so well. It is impossible to see him and not to love him. That is the common experience of the many and diverse people who have told me of their visits to his forest home."

He last left his forest retreat in 1955 to go to Benares. I believe that this journey, made at the age of 129, was the only occasion he flew in an aeroplane. He was visited by many of the most eminent philosophers and Sadhus of India. The photographs taken by Mr. Thakur Lal Manandhar show the immense vitality that carried him through that arduous undertaking.

The second time I saw him he had grown very frail. His voice had lost some of its splendid resonance, but his look was as brilliant as ever. He gave me advice of inestimable value and what is more, inspired me with the determination to carry it out. I was fortunate this time in meeting his devotee, Mr. Thakur Lal Manandhar, who has since greatly helped me and is my collaborator in writing the present book.

In 1962, his friends and devotees, among whom were a small group of English men and women who had visited him with me, did their best to arrange for him to go to Benares to avoid the rigours of the coming Himalayan winter. It was not to be. He lost the last remnants of strength, caught pneumonia and died after a short illness.

I shall finish by quoting verbatim Manandhar's letter announcing his death on the 28th of January 1963.

"Dear Mr. Bennett,
A big misfortune has fallen upon us. Our revered Shivapuri Baba departed from this world in the early morning at daybreak yesterday.

He had been suffering from an attack of flu since Thursday. His condition on Friday improved a bit after doctor's treatment. But the next day it grew worse. On Sunday the doctor gave him injection (glucose) but still his condition deteriorated and the doctor gave up all hope of recovery. Words fail to describe the manner of his death. He was fully conscious and he could even speak until the last moment. He gave his last message. These are the exact words he spoke. 'Live Right Life, Worship God. That is all. Nothing more.' At 6.15 he got up from his bed, sat down on the bed, asked for a drink, said 'I'm gone' (in Hindi 'Gaya') and laid himself down on his right as usual resting his head on the palm of his right hand and left this mortal coil. Wonderful!

A wonder among men, a King among yogis, an ideal Sannyasin is now no more with us. All homage to. him. His teaching, the rarest gift on earth, is there with us to give us Light and Hope. His last rites were performed by the local Sannyasins and visitors came in thousands to offer him their salutations.

We have been able now to arrange with the Government of Nepal for keeping the place as neat and clean as before.

His friends and admirers from all over the world can come and offer him their homage.

Stricken with sorrow at the moment I would rather end up.

With my best wishes and regards.

Yours sincerely,
Thakur Lal Manandhar."

The Great Pilgrimage was ended. On this earth and in this life it had lasted one hundred and thirty-seven years. Who can say what was needed to have been born such as he was, with a smile on his lips and God-Realization already in those wonderful ageless eyes. It is a great privilege to meet such men. They are our guarantee that the impossible is attainable, that it is possible to know All and remain for ever with that Knowledge.

CHAPTER TWO

TEACHING AND METHOD

UNLIKE most teachers, the Shivapuri Baba used no fixed form of presentation. Apart from the fundamental principles, which never varied, he suited his explanations and his language to the formation of the listener. The great majority of those who approached him for advice were Hindus, and to them he spoke in the language of the Bhagavad Gita. Speaking with Christians, he referred to the Bible and took his illustrations from the life and teaching of Christ. He was equally at home in the terminology and concepts of Sufism, so much so that when I first spoke with him, I came away with the conviction that he was a Muslim. When he quoted from the Buddhist scriptures, he did so with so evident a love towards the Buddha, that the place of Buddhism in the spiritual life of man acquired a new significance. Professor Ratnasuriya, through whom I first heard of his existence, assured me that he was, like Ramakrishna, equally at home in all religions.

But this is not all. He could speak clearly and convincingly without mention of God or the soul. He could explain the purpose of life and its fulfilment in terms of Truth, and the search for understanding, with no reference to religious worship or beliefs of any kind. He said: "If you believe in God, then your search must be for God; but even if you believe in nothing, you must still have some conviction that there is a meaning behind this visible world. You must be determined to seek out that meaning and understand it."

A score or more of people have told me about their experiences with the Shivapuri Baba. Each one said something different from all the others. This is, in my opinion, the sign of a truly enlightened Being, who does not depend upon anything that he has learned, or even that he himself has found out, but can say and do what is most appropriate to each situation that arises. With me, he spoke in a way that went direct to my problem, and did not waste time in telling me what I had already learned from my own experience or from other teachers. In order to give some idea of his extra-ordinary power to meet everyone upon their own ground, it would be necessary to describe the experiences of a large number of his pupils and visitors; in the available space I can only cite three or four.

I shall start with the account given by my collaborator and main source of the life and teachings of the Shivapuri Baba, Mr. Thakur Lal Manandhar.

"It was in November 1935 that, one morning, I left my home in a fit of dejection, since the conditioned existence I had then at home was not to my liking. But fate meant otherwise. I had to come back after a fortnight's journey up the mountains. Life seemed to me like a dungeon. A few months later, I was to witness the terrible suffering of a dying relative which all the more aggra-vated my distaste for life. In utter helplessness, my thoughts turned towards the Shivapuri Baba of whom I had heard for quite a long time. The idea came to my mind that I must go to him for help. But he was to be feared like a lion, since such was then the impression created in me by what I could gather from some of the people who had seen him. Still, I ventured to approach him.

"One fine morning in April 1936, I went to see him in Kirā-teshwar (close to the temple of Pashupati Nath) where he was then residing. I walked up stealthily from the back. The little window of his hut was left open, and through it I had my first glimpse of his splendid personality. He was sitting quite alone. When he turned towards the window, his eyes fell on me. I could not look straight at him. His eyes were so brilliant and penetrating. I was convinced that he knew everything of myself, and it seemed absurd to ask any of my questions. Tears rolled down from my eyes and I stood folding my hands. With a kindly look, he said: 'You have the book of the Gita in your pocket, don't you?' 'Yes, sir.' 'Read the first three verses of the sixteenth chapter.' Before I could read them out to him, he said again, 'Practice those twenty-six qualities or virtues described.' That was all he said. I came back home.

39

"I read the verses and their translations over and over again, but I could not make out what all those virtues really meant and wondered how they were to be applied. I was perplexed and after a few days approached him the second time. As soon as he saw me this time, he said: 'Put up a routine of your day's work with fixed duties and go ahead. Then see your success and failure in the evening.' I came back home and tried as best I could. Still I could not get at the clue. After an interval of a week, I went to see him again the third time. This time he invited me to sit before him inside the hut. It seemed he knew my difficulties and offered to help me. He said: 'You can come to me and speak about your difficulties. You are now like an infant with very little understanding. You need to develop your capabilities and grow up spiritually.' And he spoke of the necessity for a competent teacher who is self-realized. But when I said that such persons are rarely found, he replied saying that an aspirant, if he is really in earnest, naturally obtains such a guru and he will be liberated in due course. He spoke of *Yama*, *Niyama* and *Swadharma* which, according to the Hindu system of education, one must practise from early childhood, that is during the period of Brahmacharya. A fixed routine of daily life, with fixed items of duties, is required. This means that a certain code of life is to be accepted and one must abide by the laws and principles pertaining thereto, even at the risk of one's own life. This, he said, is a course that requires thirty-six years to complete. The first twelve years are to be devoted to knowing life, which he calls tattwa-jnana or relative knowledge, the next twelve years for maintaining that knowledge, and the last twelve years, for trying to realize God. The first stage he calls Self-Realization, the second Soul-Realization, and the last God-Realization. Then an elaborate description was given which was meant to give me a very broad idea of self-discipline, as it used to be practised in Ancient India, by sitting with a guru and learning things practically. Stories of Lord Krishna's discipleship under Sandipani and a host of other celebrated personalities of the Mahābhārata and the Ramayana were told, and how their mind and intelligence were controlled and developed as a result. I returned well satisfied.

"On my way back, I thought that a teacher who is a M.A., if he wishes to teach alphabet to children, must of necessity bring himself down to their level. And so it was when I remember his following speech which he then gave me:

" 'God has sent Wisdom with you. Wisdom is your friend. Wisdom plays with Desire and by their unlawful contact they gave birth to Mind. This Mind marries a girl named *Chapalatā* or Restlessness and by this he got the five senses. This Mind has got another wife too whose name is Hope and by this second wife he got two sons namely Anger and Greed. Thus a family is set up and they make a home to live in this body. This unlawful playing of Wisdom and Desire is *Avidya* or Ignorance. And in course of time, as Mind experiences fears and anxieties through the five senses, he becomes much distracted or disturbed, and then turns back to his mother Wisdom and cries for help. Wisdom then comes and consults YOU, meaning Soul, who then tells her to renounce her family and to remain in communion with YOU or Soul. This communion with Soul, is what we call Realization or *Bodha.*'

"I had my doubts as to my capability to accept a code of living as he had advised. This persisted for days, and when I visited him the next time, he started by saying that one should make a firm resolve, and, however difficult the task might be, one would succeed. I believe he could read a man's thought, since he would always begin with the very topic which I had in my mind before I could give vent to it. This time, he gave me an encouraging speech saying how a Rishi of old was told that Realization of God or Truth takes as much time and patience as it would if he began drying up an ocean with a blade of grass, and how he made up his mind and took to the enormous task ahead. What is necessary is one's determination. In this connection, he related to me the following story of a bird which is as tiny as a nut and lives near the seaside.

" 'There was a bird which was as tiny as a nut living by a sea coast. And it used to lay eggs on the beach close to the sea. But every time it discovered that its eggs had all been washed away by the ocean in high tide. And anger was born in the heart of the bird. One day, in order to recover its lost eggs, the bird thought out a plan to dry up the ocean. Forthwith with a firm determination the bird started to work out its plan. It dipped itself in the ocean and flew back to the beach to dry itself up in the sand which it did repeatedly. When this process was being repeated another of its kind came and asked, "What is this that you are doing and what for?" "I'm going to dry up the ocean to recover my eggs which now it has hidden in its bosom." "Are you really? I must recover mine as well. I must join you in this effort." So saying the second bird also did the same thing. Presently other birds too came on the scene and all joined in the attempt. Soon the number grew up to millions and billions and the terrific process was on. Soon the ocean was full of mountains. Fear was created in the heart of the ocean. At long last the ocean had to yield. What a great force it is to make a strong determination however insignificant a man may be.'

"In order to give me practical hints, he asked me to bring flowers for him every day. 'I give you a simple work,' he said, 'because you are too busy at home'. Next morning, I went to the flower market and bought a bunch of flowers for one rupee and wrapped it in my pocket handkerchief. I hung it on the handle of my bicycle and rode on to his place. As soon as I was in his presence in the little hut, I opened my parcel. He smiled and said: 'Look, your intelligence is so crude at present; what makes you spoil the flowers by packing tightly in your handkerchief? Moreover, what you have brought is too much. Look, this is our flower vase, which was in front of you, since yesterday. This flower vase cannot accommodate even one fourth of what you have brought. This is a waste of money.' I said: 'I did not have this idea that you wanted flowers for this particular vase.' 'You are thoughtless inasmuch as you did not ask me why, and you could have asked me what the flowers are meant for, and have some idea before you start to do a work. How crude is your intelligence. And also you have no idea of how to handle flowers when I see you have packed them tightly in the handkerchief, which has spoiled the shape and form of the flowers, and look, many of the stalks are broken so that they are useless to stand in the vase.'

"He then asked Madhav, his devotee, to take all the flowers to be offered in a temple nearby. Not a single flower was worth keeping in the flower vase. After listening to a long discourse on intellectual development, I came back as usual. Next morning I went to the flower market again, and bought flowers only for half a rupee. I took care not to break the stalks by holding them in my hands and rode on my bicycle.

"I presented the bundle of flowers to him as soon as I saw him. He said: 'Look, don't you see you have improved; what makes you improve? This is how one learns under a Guru.' He sorted them out to put them in the flower vase. Still the flower vase could accommodate only less than half of them. 'Look,' he said, 'why did you not make a measurement of the neck of this vase yesterday. At least you could have made some approximate measurement so as to get an idea of how many. You have improved in not wasting as much money as you did yesterday. But still your flowers are a waste. Look, only half of this is contained in the vase. Improve this tomorrow.' The stalks of my flowers were too short, which he pointed out to me, and gave me an idea of how long should be the stalk of the flowers I had to bring the next day. Next morning as usual, I went to the market and spent only one fourth of a rupee for the flowers. As soon as I presented the flowers, he said: 'Look, you have improved your intelligence. The stalks have come all right and the quantity too. Now look, as far as the quantitative side is concerned, you are perfect by some ninety per cent. Next time you should give your attention to the qualitative side. The flowers you have brought are not of good quality. You can find better quality if you get an idea of quality.'

"He then gave me a clear idea of the quality in flowers, giving me examples of physical appearances of persons who are well-nourished and well-developed, and of persons who are ill-nourished, of the different kinds of flowers available in that particular season, and so on and so forth. That day's discourse gave me a broad idea of flowers, their beauty, etc., and how and where to obtain good ones. I then tried to make friends with good gardeners, and found the best friends and the best flowers. His speeches every day, criticisms of my intelligence, and pointing out of my mistakes

43

and suggestions to improve, made me after a few months an expert in the line."

We are fortunate in thus catching a glimpse of the relationship between the Shivapuri Baba, and a seeker of the Truth who belongs to his own religion. The approach is selected from the many paths to spirituality offered by the Bhagavad Gita.

From start to finish, the teaching and guidance given to Thakur Lal was founded upon the Gita; but on a Gita expounded according to the needs of the modern world, a transformed Gita true for all beliefs and modes of life. Nearly all expositions and translations of the Gita follow the monistic interpretation of the great Shankara, and I have always felt that this tends to deprive it of application to life as we know it. A modern conception is given by Dr. S. Radhakrishnan, who says in his preface that the Gita is specially suited to answer the problem of reconciling mankind. This is the same Radhakrishnan whose meeting with the Shivapuri Baba took place later, but in many respects his translation agrees with interpretations given by our sage. Read today, after studying the teachings of the Shivapuri Baba, the Gita gains new depth and universality. It seems to express, in its own poetical language, the truths of all religions.

Leaving now the Hindu approach, I shall quote verbatim a conversation between the Shivapuri Baba and two English ladies, Melissa and Marjorie, daughters of the late Sir Charles Marston, himself a devoted seeker after the truths of Bible history. These ladies visited Kathmandu with me in 1961, and were invited to put their questions in whatever form they wished. They gave an account of their life and search. One had lost her husband after a few years of married life and had been a widow for nearly twenty years. The other had never married. They had both been interested for many years in the teachings of Gurdjieff, by which they had tried to live, and had more recently met Subud and practised the latihan. They have travelled very extensively in pursuit of a better understanding of the origins of human religions and cultures, and of the problem that troubles us all—the reason for our existence and the right way of life.

Melissa ended her account by saying: "There is always the

feeling, perhaps more in the West than in the East, of not really understanding why we are here. That our life is passing, and somehow, we are not really using it as we might."

The Shivapuri Baba, who had listened carefully to all they told him, was sitting out of doors in an armchair holding a rose in his hand. We were sitting in front of him on low stools. He smiled, held out the rose and said:

S.B. Now—so to say—there is smell in this flower. Can I explain that smell so that you will smell it yourself?

M.M. No, I suppose not.

S.B. However I explain, you cannot know the smell. If I give it in your hand and you smell it, you know what the smell is. Is that not so?

In the same way, I cannot answer your questions. Your questions will be answered only by God. See Him first. Every mystery is solved. Before that, whatever answer I can give you, it will not solve your problems. The first thing is to reach God. By seeing God, everything is known.

M.M. How can we do that?

S.B. Think of God alone. Dismiss every thought from your mind. You will see God.

These words, so commonplace when reproduced on paper, were said with such simple conviction that the answer to all problems seemed to be there, almost within reach. I remembered how deeply I had been stirred when he said the same to me a year before. The ladies also were stirred, but with feminine practicality they came out with:

M.M. That is very difficult.

S.B. It is difficult, but not impossible. It is difficult—I do know. But if you will take enough trouble to remove that difficulty, all other difficulties of life will vanish. Unless we see God, we cannot know anything. Before the sun comes, we can see nothing on the ground. When the sun comes, we see everything. So the Presence of God. When we know God we know everything. Before that, a simple explanation is no explanation at all. I can say, this is sweet smelling. But how many flowers there are that have a sweet smell! What is the nature of this smell? Unless you smell it, you cannot know. One can experience it, but it can never be explained.

45

Let the thought of God be alone in your mind, destroy every other thought. You will see God before you and all your problems are solved.

This is the first business.

Now, unless you live a disciplined life, this meditation is not possible. There is this body; you should know the requirements of this body. You will have to hear, you will have to see, you will have to sleep, you will have to taste, you will have to spit, you will have to breathe. One thousand activities are there in this body. All these activities are to be controlled and commanded. How much to eat, how much to sleep, what to see, what to hear? All this should be controlled and commanded. This is one duty.

Another duty is towards home, society, nation, etc. Find out what we have to do.

A third duty concerns material needs. Without material wealth, we cannot do these things. For that we have a professional duty.

These are the duties one has got to do. They should be found out and practised properly, without any failure, without commission or omission. Then life becomes steady. In the steady life, meditation is very easy.

At this point, the Shivapuri Baba introduced a notion that clarifies not only much that is written in the Gita, but the whole problem of consciousness, its nature and limitations. At this stage, I will quote his words without commenting, but will return to them later, when I come to the question of the significance of his teaching for our present age. Breaking off, for no apparent reason, his abstract explanation about duties, he said:

S.B. Now your body is covered with this cloth. If the cloth is removed, I can see your body. In the same way, we are covered by consciousness. God is beyond consciousness. Forget this consciousness a moment; you will see God. In a flash! First, what we have got to do is: discipline this life, then meditate on God. When you see God, every problem is solved.

From here he went on to give detailed explanations of the duties and disciplines of this life. I will give these in the fullest possible detail in a later chapter. The point I wish to bring out here is the

46

contrast in the presentation to Thakur Lal Manandhar and to the two ladies.

The latter were on a few days' visit and could not receive detailed instruction on Right Living, but their question was real and burning. He answered it directly and convincingly, on the assumption that they would see from his answer what must be added to the methods of self-surrender and self-discipline they had followed hitherto.

The third example comes from Tarzie Vittachi, probably the greatest journalist that Asia has so far produced. He was born and brought up in Ceylon in a strict Buddhist family. When he grew up, he turned against religion, and even persuaded his parents to follow him into agnosticism. He was attracted by the uncompromising unsentimentality of Gurdjieff's teaching, as presented by a pupil of Ouspensky who had emigrated to Ceylon. He eventually came to visit me about ten years ago at Coombe Springs. By a strange combination of apparent accidents, he was brought to Subud when Pak Subuh first came in 1957, and, as all his friends will testify, has been profoundly changed and developed spiritually by the practice of the latihan.

In March 1961, I wrote and asked friends in Calcutta to find out for me if the Shivapuri Baba was still alive, and whether he would allow me to visit him. I received the following letter from Tarzie a few weeks later:

"When Ian and Mariani showed me your letter, it seemed to us all that my arrival just at that time, and having two and a half days' free time, was calculated to make me undertake the journey. Besides Bapak had once said I was 'courier'. And, to make it nice and tidy, some friends of mine came over from Ceylon, Kathmandu bound, irresistibly. There were all kinds of difficulties, of course; no exchange, no visa, passport not valid for Nepal, no consulate in Calcutta to validate it, Sunday intervening, etc., etc. But we knew it would be all right in the end, and it was.

"The night I arrived in Kathmandu, I met Rawle Knox of the London Observer, who had just written a piece about an American who had arrived in Kathmandu on a round-the-world-in-40-days junket. He had contrasted this feat with that of a man in Nepal who had done the same trip, but took 40 years to do it. What was his name? Shivapuri Baba! The taxi driver and the hotel courier also knew about Shivapuri Baba, and they told me that Capt. Jai Singh, the king's chief pilot, who lived at the Royal Hotel where I stayed, was a disciple.

"So I went to see Shivapuri Baba the next afternoon in his forest retreat. I was a little apprehensive about hunting a man down in a forest, being no Trader Horn, but it was quite different from what I imagined. The forest is actually a beautifully kept wood, and had the most wonderful sense of peace about it. There was nothing of the grimness you feel in a Ceylon jungle.

"He was seated in the sun in his garden and there was a stool and cigarettes ready for me because I had been expected.

"He was a dishevelled old-old man with the happiest smile I have ever seen on an adult's face. His old eyes gleamed in welcome. I asked him if I could speak in English. He speaks it almost impeccably. I said I'd come in response to a letter from you, that you'd expressed a wish to visit him in March; that you'd heard that he'd spoken about Bapak.

"He replied that you would be very welcome; you need not write to him—just come. He had heard about Subud 'in Indonesia' and had read a book about Subud (presumably yours). I asked whether he could tell me anything about his feeling about Subud, which I felt you were keen on finding out, and he replied 'I will speak about that when Mr. Bennett comes, with him.'

"I asked whether he could tell me anything about Bapak, and he said 'It is not right to talk about others but this I will say: He will take you to Pure Consciousness. From there you will be able to see your way to Truth, God, clearly, without anyone else's help.'

"I asked him how we could strengthen our spiritual life and how we could escape being drawn back constantly into politics, emotions, passions and everything irrelevant to the religious life.

"His reply was: 'Man has three duties:

Physical duty—the obligations he was born to; earning a living, acquitting himself and his talents in the world, looking after his dependents and so on.

48

Moral duty—to be aware of the obligation towards oneself to seek the Truth for twenty-four hours of the day.

Spiritual duty—Worship of God—but this we will appreciate only later. Attention to the first two duties—taken very simply, will take us far along the way.

" 'In one *decade* a man who attends to the first two duties will be able to clean his mind and ask only for Truth and the Way of God.

" 'You must not cease working at these two duties even for one minute. A minute's lapse will cause emotions, passions, thoughts to invade your mind.'

"I asked how they could be kept out.

" 'Again take it very simply' he said. 'People come to your home to visit you. You give them tea and whisky. They will come again because they know they will be welcome. If you don't *entertain* them they will drop you and go elsewhere. Like my house here. There is a barbed wire round it. Only people I want to let in may come in. And the only qualification is *interest* to come in here. Others are not let in or entertained. Put a barbed wire fence round your mind.'

"Then he said a most remarkable thing. 'If you cannot pay attention to these two duties you might as well adopt a Religion!'

"Some people in Nepal say he is 500 years old. Sceptics say he is only 200. He himself said he was born in 1826.

" 'By the practice of Brahmacharya it is possible to live to a great age,' he said.

"He gave me some personal advice: 'Decide how much you want. Decide how many friends, how many people you want to see; how much money you need to earn to live with your family, how much time you will give to thinking and talking about things like journalism, politics and other things; how much food and drink and entertainment you feel you need. Then stick to this regimen as best you can. Don't let yourself be carried beyond these limits.'

"At this point I felt he needed rest.

"Is it time for me to go? I asked.

" 'Yes,' he said, adding: 'Bring any friends you wish. Only, they must be interested.' " That is the end of Tarzie's letter.

49

When I myself visited him a few months later, I did not ask him outright for his opinion of Subud. Such questioning seems indelicate for it calls for approval or condemnation, either of which attitudes are foreign to the perfected man. He was asked in my presence of a certain well-known Indian yogi whether he had attained God-Realization or not. He gave no sign of approval or disapproval, but said only: 'He is on the way to it.' His reply to Tarzie Vittachi about Pak Subuh was all that I could hope for.

He did, however, give a very valuable, though indirect, commentary upon Subud in replying to two sisters. The first occasion was in 1961 when he was asked:

H.C. Is preparation necessary? In the deep meditation we have learned from the Maharshi and also in Subud, we have been told that no preparation is necessary, and that it is possible to reach God-Realization by the practice of the meditation or the latihan and nothing else. What would you say to this, Babaji?

S.B. To imagine that one can reach God-Consciousness without preparation is like expecting to buy an elephant for two pice.

H.C. And yet we have seen that people who come without any preparation do make progress in these exercises.

S.B. If so, then the exercise itself becomes the preparation. Without preparation, that is, without a strong mind, meditation is impossible.

J.G.B. Some rare people are born with a gift for the spiritual life. They go right ahead without the years of preparation that others find necessary.

S.B. If someone is born with spiritual preparation, they must have acquired it by the discipline they practised in previous lives. Also you must understand that many bad habits are formed in this life. Until these bad habits are removed, meditation is impossible. Without these bad habits, it would not take so long.

H.C. But we have been told that no discipline is necessary; that all will come by itself from practice of the spiritual exercises.

S.B. There is some misunderstanding here. Everyone knows that without discipline the spiritual life is impossible.

The following year the ladies, whose questions have already

been mentioned, asked him about discipline and spiritual exercises in connection with human relationships.

M.M. I was going to ask you, please, about Subud; because we are rather disturbed amongst the people in Subud, that it has not made for more unity amongst us. Instead, there is almost what I would call 'forceful disunity' occurring amongst our newer friends in Subud. It is very difficult for us to work together. Why is this? Is it just a phase we are going through?

S.B. It is owing to this; no practice of moral discipline, so these things happen.

J.G.B. You mean that we practice the latihan, but we do not practise moral discipline.

S.B. Yes. Practise moral discipline. Then it is very easy, these charities etc. Before you study chemistry, you cannot study medicine. Before you study mathematics, you cannot do engineering. So, before you practise these moral disciplines, it is not possible to have true meditation.

Now, I sit here. If this seat will go on vibrating, I cannot sit properly. It should be steady. Meditation is through mind. If mind is shaking, one cannot meditate properly. In a pool of water, you look, your face is seen clear. Throw a stone in the water or something; when there are waves, your image is not seen clear. So, when there is this liking, disliking, anger and various other natures, meditation is not possible.

J.G.B. Yet, we are told that by the practice of the latihan alone, the mind will become steady automatically. Pak Subuh says that the mind must do nothing but submit to the Power of God, then it is the Power of God that will make the mind steady.

S.B. That is a fancy saying. To a certain extent, of course, the mind will become steady; but not practically. Discipline is necessary. When there is no cause, you will be quiet. When some causes come, that quietness will break and you will come forward with your original nature. When there will be no wind, the leaves will be steady. When there is a little bit of wind, they will begin to shake. So it is when anything will go against you, or come in favour of you: this quietness will break.

J.G.B. Unless you have discipline?

S.B. Yes. Unless the virtues are well practised, this latihan will not give fruit.

I will end this chapter with an account of my own experiences. I only met the Shivapuri Baba on two occasions, at Easter 1961 and 1962. Each time I had several conversations with him alone, as well as meetings with others.

In our private talks, he went straight to the point: I spent too much of my time and energy upon duties that were not essential; I could hope to come quickly to the knowledge of God if only I were to arrange my life better and devote more time to meditation. Whatever had been undertaken must be carried through, but if I would, from that time on, set myself to avoid commitments that would take time from meditation, I would soon find myself in an entirely different situation.

When I spoke to him about various experiences, I saw that he understood and could evaluate them without hesitation. For example, I referred to the joyful state that one reaches when thoughts and feelings are quiet and the inward vision begins to open. He said: "That joyful feeling is an obstacle. There must be neither joy nor suffering in meditation, only an intense desire to see God."

His insistence upon the supreme importance of attaining the Beatific Vision seemed to me to underrate the aspect of service in our life on earth. I had always felt this to be a defect in the Indian conception of life. I doubted that the belief in personal God-Realization as the greatest, and indeed the sole valid aim of human existence, could be found in the original Vedic religion. I had never felt at home with the Indian systems of philosophy or even with the practice of Yoga (except as physical exercise) in so far as these repudiate the world as unreal and unworthy of our interest.

I put the question to the Shivapuri Baba roughly in the following words:

J.G.B. Babaji, you teach the need for the threefold discipline, but you place the attainment of the knowledge of God at the summit. This, of course, I am sure is true—but I want to ask you if there does not still remain a task to be performed. Surely the knowledge of God, must mean the knowledge of God's Will, that is Dharma. If so, does not Dharma remain even after the supreme realization. Would not a man who has attained perfect knowledge and power have the obligation to use them for serving the Divine Purpose?

S.B. The Dharma is the same as the duties. These duties have to be performed. They are our service to God. There is no other.

J.G.B. I have various responsibilities. I am a student and a writer, and I have a place near London called Coombe Springs where people come who are searching for the Truth. They expect me to help them as far as I am able. Are these activities to be regarded as duties which I should perform, or should I be free from them?

S.B. You should be free. But you have accepted these obligations. They must be fulfilled without commission or omission. It is the same with marriage. You are married and have children. You must perform your duties as a married man. But these should be performed in such a way as not to hinder your search for God. Little by little, you will be able to diminish them. First professional duties are to be reduced to what is necessary, then family duties. Finally, there remains only the duty to preserve the existence of your body.

Nevertheless, even now you can meditate upon God and the meaning of life. Every day you must set aside as much time as you can for this, and you will come to it.

J.G.B. This I do see; but still I remain doubtful about the treatment of the task of serving God and our fellow men—as something of minor significance—a concession to the weakness of mind that prevents us from devoting ourselves every hour of the day to the inner search, with no other object than to find Truth. I cannot believe that man was given such diverse and such extraordinary powers of action on this earth, unless there was a very high purpose to be served.

S.B. The highest purpose is served by the simple performance of our duties. That is Dharma. This is no easy matter. The duties cannot be recognized and performed properly, unless there is a keen intelligence. Then it is necessary to have a strong mind in order to meditate without wavering upon God. In order to acquire a strong mind there must be moral discipline. Therefore, all three are necessary: duty, discipline and devotion.

J.G.B. Forgive me, Babaji, if I press the question.

S.B. You must do so. You have come to me to get your doubts removed. For that you must press your questions.

J.G.B. May I take the case of Shankarāchārya. He is the great exponent of the Vedanta of absolute monism. His saying: *Brahma satyam jagan mithya jīvo Brahmaiva nāparah*—Brahman is real, the world is a sham, the Jiwa is none other than Brahman itself. Nevertheless, Shankara who died, they say, at the early age of thirty-two, was the most active and effectual man of his day, and one of the most extraordinary reformers of any age. He not only wrote forty or fifty important books, but travelled the length and breadth of India engaging in disputes. He founded ten great monastic orders, of which four are still active, and in one of which you yourself were initiated. He combatted the errors of Buddhism and other heretical sects on the one hand, and on the other kept in check the tendency towards a rigid authoritarianism in the revival of Brahmanism. How could it be said that such a man looked upon the world as a sham that should be disregarded by the wise man in search of Truth?

S.B. You have not understood how to discriminate between Absolute and Relative. I also spent forty years travelling round the world. I did not do this for nothing, but because it was a duty to be fulfilled. I met thousands of people, most of whom asked me questions about God and the meaning of life. I answered them as I answer you now, because it is my professional duty. You also have professional duties that you must fulfil. If these are rightly chosen, they are your Dharma.

At the same time, you must understand that all this does not lead to God. It is the condition for being able to search for God: but that search is a different matter. Shankara said that Brahman alone is real, but he did not say that man has no duties in this world. On the contrary, he devoted his life to making clear what were the duties of people of his time. He lived more than a thousand years ago, and now the situation is changed. Nothing remains the same in this world, and so there can be no permanent rules, which fix the duties once and for all. Therefore, you have to study the conditions of life and choose your duties accordingly. You have a keen intelligence, and you have to study the conditions of life in England, so that you can show your pupils what their duties should be now.

But this must not prevent you from devoting the necessary time for meditation. You must not allow the relative to overcome the absolute in you. When you allow that, life becomes a sham and an illusion. That is all.

This conversation, reproduced from memory, fails to convey the brilliant light that the old man shed on every subject he touched. He made me see that the conflict between monists and dualists is not one of substance, but of emphasis. In the presence of the infinite, the finite does not count. As we were taught at school, infinity is not increased by adding to it, or diminished by subtraction. So the contact with Infinity, which is the Beatific Vision or God-Realization, is neither enhanced nor tarnished by anything in the world. In this sense it is true to say with Shankara: Brahman alone is Real, the world is a sham. But it is also true to say that without the finite we could not know the infinite.

The beauty of the Shivapuri Baba's exposition is that the philosophical and the practical problems are not separated. The aim is to know God—that is Infinity. But in order to know, one must *be able* to know. To be able, means to be strong, and without discipline strength cannot be achieved. Again, "God doth not need either man's work or His own gifts." And yet He requires of us that we should not be hearers only, but doers of the Word.

The enigma of the finite and the infinite is always with us. The Vedanta does not remove it. No one has preached a more thoroughgoing monism than Shankara. No one practised a more thoroughgoing dualism. The Shivapuri Baba cuts the Gordian knot in the simplest way by saying that both are right, but *neither is right without the other.*

Although this explanation is magnificent in its combination of uncompromising devotion to the Infinity of God and commonsense acceptance of experience as we find it, there remained for me the question of the Divine Purpose. It seems to me that for an

Indian this is a meaningless question. The idea of purpose is incompatible with any thoroughgoing monism. This is one reason, no doubt, why the historical sense is so seldom found among Indian thinkers.

Another factor is the immense influence that the Buddha has had upon Indian thought. Although Buddhism as a religion has disappeared from India, its founder is still regarded as one of the greatest of Indian thinkers and reformers. Now, the Buddha founded his doctrine on the principle of causality, *nidāna* expressed in the famous formula: "From the arising of this, that cometh to be; and from the cessation of this, that ceaseth to be."

This doctrine precludes purposeful action in the creative sense, and strengthens the hold on men's minds of the feeling that the world is a cold place from which we should seek to make our escape as quickly as possible. Lest we should suppose that the 'world' means just this earthly existence, the Buddha—so far as we can judge from the discourses that have been preserved—returned again and again to the theme that the divine Beings in heaven are no better off than we are, inasmuch as they also remain bound by the chains of causality.

When I asked the Shivapuri Baba if the perfected man who had attained God-Realization had any further goal before him, or other task to be performed, he was quite emphatic. "That is the end; that is the final goal."

That is how we left it when I took my leave of him in April 1961. I did not see him again for a year, and during this time my doubts about his explanation continued to haunt me. The next time I saw him, in April 1962, he had grown much weaker and at last looked like an old, old man near to death. Nevertheless, his intelligence was as keen as ever and he was quite ready to answer my questions.

I again said to him that I could not accept the notion that the perfected man has no further work to do except to protect his body. This time, he answered in a different and unexpected way by speaking to me about myself.

S.B. I see that you are now nearer to the moment when you will

56

see God. I can now promise you that you will come to this vision before you die. If you will set yourself free from so many duties, and give yourself more time for meditation, you will come to it quickly: perhaps within two years. When you come to that you will know the answer for yourself.

J.G.B. I have decided to enter the Roman Catholic Church later this year. Would you say that worship in the form of the Christian sacraments is an obstacle to the Realization you promise me?

S.B. No. It is right for you. You must use all means you can. Make much use of the Rosary. It will help you when your mind cannot stand the strain of the pure meditation without form.

If you will persist, you will see God. Christ will come to you and show you. That is how you should meditate. Sometimes with the help of the Rosary or an Image or Picture, sometimes meditate on the nature of Christ; but whenever you are strong enough, put all forms and images away and think of God without name or form.

J.G.B. I have sometimes felt myself very near to this Realization, but my mind is too weak to keep all other thoughts away.

S.B. You must not have any doubts that you will come to it. Be sure that if you ask enough, God will come.

J.G.B. I still cannot imagine that such a realization is the end of the journey. There must still be work to be done.

S.B. In one sense it is the end of the journey. In another sense it is not so. You see that I live here and perform my duties. My speaking with you now is a duty which I must perform.

J.G.B. But is that all? Does not the world need help from those who have seen God and have been filled with His Grace?

The answer he gave to this question was a complete surprise, but it seemed like the inevitable conclusion to be drawn from all that he had said before.

S.B. When you come to that Realization, you will know God and you will enter into God and be one with God. Then you will become what Christ was from the beginning. When you have entered into God, you may return into this world. But then you will come like Christ came to help the needs of the world. But all this you cannot know yet: you will only know it when you come to that Realization. You will come to that before you die—that I can

57

promise you—but how soon you will come I cannot say. It depends upon the way you follow the advice I have given you.

Such a conversation could not fail to have a profound effect upon me. Indeed, I know of no one who has spoken seriously with him who has not come away with new understanding, and a new resolve to pursue more strenuously the search for Truth. When I took leave of him, I knew that we should not meet again, but I also knew that what I had received from him would never leave me. There is no question of a personal relationship: he is beyond all human ties.

Among the many changes in my understanding brought about by my talks with him—indeed by the simple effect of his presence— I am aware of a new warmth of feeling towards India and Indian spirituality.

I have never been able to accept the claim made by fervent admirers of the great Indian saints and sages of our time, that India is pre-eminent in spirituality above all other countries and peoples of the world. This claim is expressed, for example, by that remarkable and holy man Sri Aurobindo in his book *The Yoga and its Objects* (1931): "God always reserves to Himself a chosen country where the higher knowledge is preserved unbroken, by the masses and by the *élite* alike, through all the perils and vicissitudes. And, in our age, or at any rate for the present series of four *Yugas*, that country is India."

This does not mean that I doubted the reality of Indian spiritual life and experience. I have seen enough of it myself to know how sincere is the devotion of Indians to the spiritual ideal. But I have always felt a certain unpracticality, a tendency to seek for the taste of Reality, rather than its fruition in practical Life. I do not mean by this that the great spiritual leaders of India have been unpractical men. Shankara was a shining example of practical realism in his time, and so in our own day have been Gandhi and Radhakrishnan. Nor is Indian spirituality so other-worldly as to have no care for suffering humanity. Vivekananda and the Ramakrishna Mission, and all the more recent welfare organizations, are the modern expression of *Dāna*, or charity, that is one of the basic duties of the Indian spiritual life.

My difficulties were of another kind. They came from my inability to find evidence of concreteness in Indian thought, of a historical sense in the interpretation of human experience, and a general tendency to prefer grand but vague speculations to practical realities. My contact with the Shivapuri Baba removed many of these difficulties. I saw in him a man concrete and clear in his thinking, an enemy of speculation, and eminently practical, both in his actions and in the advice he gives to others. But far more than all this, I saw in him a perfected human being who had left far behind him all the struggles and anxieties of the world, and who, though completely free from the need to do anything whatsoever, was nevertheless infinitely patient and long-suffering in helping those who came to him with a genuine desire to be helped.

Looking at India from the perspective of his remote hermitage, nearly a thousand miles across the great sub-continent from his birthplace in Kerala, I saw it with different eyes. India is in the throes of a conflict between the old spirituality and the new materialism. As the Shivapuri Baba said to Thakur Lal, it is Wisdom playing with Desire, and out of it a new Mind will be born. The Mind of India will make an indispensable contribution to the spiritualization of mankind that is now in progress. From that Mind, all the world will profit, but India must also be prepared to learn and to accept the reality of spiritual insights that are totally different from its own.

In this sense, the Shivapuri Baba was a forerunner of the New Epoch, for he could understand Christian and Muslim spirituality and he could read the signs of the times. He warned us that a great change is coming over the world, but he also showed us how to prepare for it.

In the next chapters, I shall endeavour to piece together the fragments of his teaching, using Manandhar's notes and the records of my own talks with him.

CHAPTER THREE

RIGHT LIFE

THE Shivapuri Baba's entire teaching can be summed up in the words: Right Life. They correspond to the Sanskirt *Swadharma*; but characteristically, he invests them with a wider and stronger meaning than is customary. Dharma, in ordinary talk, means the observances required by one's religion and caste. In philosophy, it stands for the cosmic order or absolute rightness. Much more than either of these is implied in the Shivapuri Baba's doctrine of Right Life.

Above all, it stands for completeness, for a life lived upon all levels and in all departments. It comprises the three disciplines bodily, moral and spiritual referred to in the conversation with Radakrishnan, but it does not remain within the limits of embodied existence, but leads on to Moksha or Final Liberation of the Self.

There is a tendency to regard the three disciplines as an ordered sequence, through which the soul has to pass, or else to look upon the bodily and moral disciplines as nothing more than preparation for the Spiritual Life. The Shivapuri Baba treats all three as a timeless Reality into which the soul enters and finds its home. The aim and goal is God-Realization: but this is not the end in one sense only—that of the Beatific Vision in which the Soul meets with God. As the Bhagavad Gita teaches in the 9th and 10th Chapters, God manifests in all his Creation and we can meet Him everywhere. The only difference is in the degree of direct contact. In the world, we meet God veiled in Māyā, but it is God nonetheless Who is the Source of even the pleasures of sense. Thus Self-Realization is God-Realization with a very different meaning from that given by the Vedantins. Sukha or pleasure is a meeting with God, Who though veiled is nevertheless the Love that arouses the passion of the lover. Shanti or Peace is not only the prerequisite for seeing God face to face: it is also the bliss which crowns the discipline of the Spirit.

The error of man is to prefer the veiled to the Revealed, the twilight of illusion to the Light of Reality. Providing everything is given its rightful place, all is legitimate. Nay more, all is necessary for the completeness of Right Living.

Thus Right Living leads to the fulfilment of the four ends of human existence.*

Traditionally, Swadharma is the rule of life prescribed by one's caste, sex, age, spiritual aspirations and the external conditions of one's life. The Shivapuri Baba does not reject this interpretation, but brings it up-to-date so that it can be applied to our own lives; including those of Western people who have no caste, and whose outward conditions of existence are totally different from those of the Indian tradition.

I shall introduce the notion of Right Life by quoting from a conversation between a Hindu visitor and the Shivapuri Baba.

Q. Sir, why are we so unhappy?

S.B. Because you don't live the Right Life.

Q. What is the Right Life?

S.B. It is a life with some definite aim. It is a planned and discriminative life, with duties necessary and helpful for achieving the aim in the shortest possible time.

Q. What is the greatest aim of life?

S.B. To see Truth.

Q. Why should we want to see Truth?

S.B. Because before that we cannot be omnipotent, omniscient, and omnipresent.

Q. What are the chief elements of the Right Life?

S.B. Discrimination and devotion.

Q. Please explain them.

S.B. You see that for maintaining body, you have to discharge certain duties towards nature, towards family, towards society, towards government and towards profession. All these should be

---

* These are *dharma* or right living, *artha* or wealth, *kama* or satisfaction of desires and *moksha* or liberation. The first three are regarded as means whereby a man can attain the fourth.

planned and done with dexterity. Then for making your mind strong you have to cultivate virtues, charity, self-control, fearlessness, patience, together with the rest of the twenty-six virtues described in the sixteenth chapter of the Gita.* This is discrimination. The rest of the time you should devote to thinking of Truth in various ways without feeling monotonous. This is Devotion. The most important thing is to see that you do not waste your time on any other work.

Q. How can we best help the world?

S.B. By living the Right Life and practising charity; mental, verbal, bodily, and pecuniary. Mentally, we should wish well even to our so-called enemies. We should not speak words likely to hurt others. We should, when possible, try to serve others physically. Then at least ten per cent of our income should be devoted to charity. This, again, should be divided into three parts. One part should go to poor spiritual aspirants and institutions for spiritual life. Another part should go to deserving cultural people and institutions. The third part should go to poor people and institutions for helping them. If people practise charity well where can there be disorder in the world?

Q. When shall we realize Truth?

S..B. When you can continuously and concentratedly ask the question 'What is Truth' or do the like, for one *muhoorta*, that is, forty-eight minutes.

Q. Some say that we must give up life in order to realize Truth?

S.B. Yes, but giving up life does not mean merely going to a forest or a cave. Even Buddha, after realizing Truth, said that it is not necessary to do that. One can realize Truth even at home if one lives the Right Life. Giving up life means giving up craving for name and fame and enjoyments.

Now let us see how he speaks to Europeans. In 1961, he agreed to send a tape-recording of a talk about his teaching for the benefit of people in England who could not come and visit him. I put questions to him that had been sent out by friends of mine and he replied.

* See pp. 95–96 for a fuller description and explanation of the twenty-six virtuous actions.

J.G.B. What is the fundamental principle of life which man should follow. What is the true life for man on this earth?

S.B. There is this body. It has many requirements. You should know the right activities for each part of the body. These right activities are to be selected and performed without any commission or omission. Another thing is mind. Mind is ruled by emotions. Mind should be ruled by reason. Calmness must prevail in the mind. The third thing is: the rest of the time should be utilized for meditating on God, to know the meaning of Life, or to see God personally. This is Right Life.

J.G.B. This duty—does it have different forms inward and outward—or is it connected only with the body?

S.B. It is connected with the body only.

J.G.B. Does our duty concern only the care of one's own body, or is there a duty towards other people as well?

S.B. Towards our own home, towards our immediate society, and towards the whole nation as well.

J.G.B. Is that all?

S.B. One duty towards body, another duty comes from our obligations towards home and society and there is another—the professional duty. One must have wealth to perform the other duties.

J.G.B. Does that third duty depend upon one's own powers and capacities? How does the child learn this duty. From parents and teachers or from himself?

S.B. By a combination of both. Parents and teachers should prepare the way. They are the agents of the Self.

J.G.B. I suppose this professional duty starts at the age of eighteen or twenty when training for life is complete.

S.B. When he reaches the age of five.

J.G.B. Five? Does reason exist at that age?

S.B. Even before reason comes; it is good that this be established.

J.G.B. May we return to the first duty—towards one's body? I suppose this includes eating, sleeping and other natural functions. How are their needs to be learned?

S.B. By studying the needs of the body. All these should be just for the maintenance of the body. Eating should be for the maintenance of the body. In the same way, sleeping, seeing, hearing, touching, feeling, spitting, passing urine, and various duties. All these duties should be fixed in time, and done without any mistake.

J.G.B. Should these duties all be taught to children?

S.B. Yes.

J.G.B. How should I act with my own children? Should they be told how to eat—not too fast, not too much, not to be ruled by like and dislike and then left to do it by themselves; or should they be shown in detail and made to learn?

S.B. You should tell them, you should explain to them clearly these things. When they go wrong, you will have to point it out to them.

J.G.B. So that from childhood, a boy or a girl should be all the time preparing, so that duties become quite clear to them?

S.B. Yes.

J.G.B. For the people who have not had the fortune to be prepared in that way, then they must learn it in after life?

S.B. Yes.

J.G.B. As regards the other duty now—the one towards society—there is always a tendency that one does this from one's heart or one's feelings. One naturally loves one's wife and children by feeling, but you say that this should be done from reason?

S.B. Yes.

J.G.B. Where does reason come from?

S.B. From experience, by experience, reason comes.

J.G.B. You mean by putting one experience against another. Confronting past and present experience?

S.B. No.

J.G.B. But reason does not come by simple experience alone.

S.B. Now. Suppose I tell you to prepare tea. You prepare it. There may be some mistakes—the real taste will not come. There may be more sugar, or more tea. Or the art of boiling may be wrong, the ingredients may be wrong. Today, you make, you taste it, and the right thing has not come. Find out the mistake today, and remedy it tomorrow. Another mistake may come. Remedy it the day after tomorrow. In this way, go on preparing that one thing for a long time. You will get the correct taste one day, then maintain the correct taste. This is reason.

J.G.B. That is very clear. By experience you mean reiterated practice and correction?

S.B. Yes. In the same way each and every duty must be studied. Until we find the right answer we must repeat and repeat. By the observation of yesterday, you can change today. By changing today, tomorrow will be different.

J.G.B. That reminds me of a saying of Gurdjieff's: 'With the present repair the past and prepare the future.'

S.B. Exactly so! Is that convincing?

J.G.B. Very convincing for those of us who have tried to live that way. Does it apply to all the three duties: towards one's body, one's family, and one's profession?

S.B. What we must do for our family we are obliged to do. Suppose we fail there, their affection will be less for us. If we do according to their requirements, they will be heartened by us and will begin to love us more and more. In the same way, we should care for neighbours also. We should be very helpful to them, never be harmful to them. They will always be eternal friends. Whenever we are in difficulty, they will come and help us. It is the same with society and nation and with all human beings. That is right life.

J.G.B. All that you have said so far amounts to this: that man should live on the earth a normal, well-balanced life in accordance with all natural laws. I take it that this is just a foundation: what is to be built upon the foundation?

S.B. No. It is separate in itself. This right life should be lived for its own sake. When all this is done, one will have a very healthy body, one will have useful friends to help, and one will have sufficient wealth and material to live on. And life will be very pleasant.

J.G.B. But man does not live for pleasure.

S.B. One should not live for pleasure; but, if it comes, it should not be rejected also. Pleasure will give satisfaction if it is accepted without being sought for.

J.G.B. After these duties, what prepares in man the necessary qualifications to come to the spiritual life?

S.B. That is to be separately studied.

J.G.B. How does man acquire these qualifications?

S.B. That God is to be seen, then only life will be all right. The meaning of life is to be known. Then only one can be happy here. To know that meaning or to see God, his thoughts should always centre round that one subject. Every other subject must vanish from the mind.

J.G.B. But can man do that without some degree of moral perfection?

S.B. Moral perfection is totally certain; it must be essential.

J.G.B. It is essential. Does this come simply by wanting God, or by discipline and self-correction?

S.B. One should not yield to liking and disliking. One should not have any other desire, other than living this life or finding out God. Then this lower nature should not play in the mind; anger and various other things.

J.G.B. They belong to our lower nature.

S.B. Yes, higher nature should be perfectly established; with its qualities like fearlessness, straightforwardness, etc. Higher nature should be cultivated in the mind. Opposite nature should be eliminated from the mind.

J.G.B. And this by a practice of self-correction or self-discipline? How is this?

S.B. Simply by seeing our behaviour. If behaviour is wrong, one should determine now that such behaviour should not be. Today anger came, tomorrow it should not come.

J.G.B. In thought, word and deed; in all three?

S.B. Yes. This moral discipline is only in thought. Physical discipline is in action.

J.G.B. You mean that one has to conquer anger in one's thoughts, it is no use to try and conquer it by one's actions.

S.B. No, it will not be.

J.G.B. If I have angry thoughts, it is not enough to stop my angry words? The thoughts are still there, the thoughts come before the actions.

S.B. Yes.

J.G.B. This is the same as the Christian teaching.

S.B. Yes. One should cultivate all the Creation as the Image of God, the Manifestation of God—one should always be humbled, humiliated before that When such thoughts are established, anger will not come.

At this point, the ladies who were with me had either grown tired of listening or else the last remarks of the Shivapuri Baba had struck a chord. One of them broke in with:

M.H. Where does this tiresome 'lower nature' come from? Is it something that humanity is growing out of?

S.B. It is inside the mind. It is the contents of the mind.

M.H. Did God make man like that?

S.B. When we cultivate, the grains come up and the weeds also will come along with them. Now, we take out all these weeds and keep only that grain. In the same way, this good nature and bad nature are the ingredients of the mind. They come up automatically. We have to suppress the impulses that come from the lower nature.

M.H. Can you tell us a little more how to see God?

S.B. Have you understood the duties of the body?

M.H. Yes, I think I can see that.

S.B. These duties you will have to plan. For that, Intelligence is indispensable. If you cannot do it for yourself you must find a teacher who will help you.

The second discipline is of the Mind. Mind is wild. Various passions, various thoughts are playing in the mind. Now these passions, these thoughts are all to be removed from the mind. One should not yield to liking and disliking. In that way, the mind will become strong. One should cultivate the higher nature. One should destroy the lower nature. This is moral discipline.

Then the mind becomes very strong. In that strong mind, when you have finished these duties for a time, you can meditate upon God. Either your mind should remain with these duties, or it should remain with God. It should have no other place.

That is the right way of life today.

M.H. What are the qualities by which we can recognize the two natures?

S.B. That you will find in the Gita. Mr. Bennett will explain all that to you. For example: fearlessness is higher nature. Fear is lower nature. Crookedness is lower nature, straightforwardness is higher nature. There are some thirty or thirty-two such qualities. Moral discipline means to incorporate all the qualities of the higher nature.

J.G.B. In one's mind?

S.B. Yes. Then mind becomes strong. One should have no liking, one should have no disliking. Reason must prevail.

Suppose you like me: you will give me everything. Suppose you hate me: you will give me nothing. This is under the influence of liking and disliking. Under the influence of reason, what will you do? You will see if I deserve or not. Suppose I am your enemy; still, if I deserve, you will give me. Suppose I am your friend; if I do not deserve, you will not give me.

This is the direction of reason. This reason must always prevail. Liking and disliking must perish.

M.H. That is very difficult.

S.B. Difficult yes. But practice will bring you to it. I can give you a decade—ten to twelve years. You can become perfect in this in ten or twelve years.

M.H. I do see that we must struggle with our lower nature. We have always been taught this. Fear especially!

S.B. (to J.G.B.) You will have to explain these things clearly to them so that they can come to the Right Life.

M.M. here intervened:

M.M. I want to ask you, Babaji, how can one make the idea of God stronger in oneself.

S.B. That should come with desire. One should desire, then one will get it.

Here Babaji asked me some question about my life, and I said that from my youth I had seen that no kind of worldly success would satisfy me. My friends said that I had wasted my life, for I had been expected to do great things but had accomplished very little. What use is it to seek results which by their very nature must perish!

S.B. Such ideas should be retained, then love for God will be intense. The attraction for worldly things must vanish. You know there was a Rishi named Yajnyavalkhya?

J.G.B. Yes. I have read his story in the Upanishad.

68

S.B. He had two wives. In the end, he wanted to go to the forest. He divided his property and gave it to his two wives. The younger wife was saying: 'O! will this property bring God to me?' 'No, it will bring worldly happiness to you,' he said. 'I don't want this. I will come along with you. I want God.'

Desire for happiness in life is bad. God alone is good for life. Then reduce the love for life. Love of God will automatically increase.

J.G.B. My experience of life has taught me to accept whatever comes and not look for everything. If it is pleasant to enjoy it. If it is painful to remember that there can be no pleasure without pain. Life is much simpler when one understands that pleasure and pain must always balance.

S.B. It is so. Pains will come, pleasures will come. Ordinary people will try to remove these pains and maintain these pleasures. Their whole work will be useless, because pain will come: one cannot avoid it.

Therefore let pains come or pleasures come; we should be indifferent to both. We should see whether we have fulfilled our duty or not. We should not see whether pleasures or pains are coming.

M.M. May I ask here a question about suffering? I have an old friend in England who is much troubled by this. She sees it for herself. She is old and has much trouble and sickness to endure. She feels that she can never get an answer to the question: why is there suffering in the world?

S.B. Now. We live in this country. We will have to obey all the rules and regulations of the Government. If we do not obey, we shall have to go to the prison. In the same way, when one lives in this body, there are some rules and regulations one will have to follow. One does not know, one breaks all these rules and regulations and suffering comes. Now there is a law for taking meals. Out of taste, one will disobey this law. One will eat more or one will eat less, one will eat unwanted articles. Here disease will come in the body, and that is suffering.

J.G.B. But even a great Saint, like Ramakrishna, died from cancer.

S.B. Yes. These bodily diseases, they will come. Suffering; it comes from sin. It is out of that. Already you know in your Christian religion, man is born with sin! Original Sin.

J.G.B. Yes, it is not only from our own personal sin; but from the fact that the whole of mankind has turned away from God and broken His law, that we have to come under the law of sin and with it the law of suffering.

S.B. Yes. But if we live this right life, with these disciplines, sufferings will be very, very much less. Many sufferings will go away. But still some sufferings will remain, that one should not mind. One should have a law of the mind to follow.

J.G.B. So the real question, Babaji, is not what is the origin of suffering, but what is the origin of sin? This is a more difficult question to answer.

S.B. Yes, but the thing is this: until we know God, we cannot get to the final answer. A simple answer may be this—because we live in a wild way, not in a civilized way.

J.G.B. But where did it start? God did not make man so that he should sin, did he?

S.B. It started out of desire to enjoy life. Yes.

J.G.B. It is a difficult question all the same.

S.B. That is why to know this question fully, unless we know God, we cannot. Today we can only say this: our desire to enjoy life brought this.

J.G.B. There are some things which you, Babaji, must be able to see from your vision which you cannot speak about. Even if you wanted to, you could not tell us.

S.B. I cannot. Words cannot reach this. Words cannot reach.

J.G.B. Therefore, if we wish to know what you know, we have to come by the same path that you have come by.

S.B. Experience alone will teach you—experience is beyond explanation.

J.G.B. We have been here eight days, and we never saw Himal. We thought we would go away without seeing the snow mountains. Today, it became clear, and we saw the mountains; and we were saying, as we were coming, the mountains have been there every day, but only on the last day we saw them. It is like that with God.

S.B. It is like that.

J.G.B. The Truth is always there; one day the clouds will go.

S.B. We are always obstructed by consciousness. Suppose you dip yourself in water—above, below and around you, you see water, nothing else. If you raise your head from the water, you will see the world outside. In the same way, we are drowned within consciousness. When we raise our knowledge, our thought beyond this consciousness, we see God at once. Forgetfulness of this consciousness for a single moment, you will see God.

J.G.B. Is this consciousness the same as what is called, in the Gita, the Kshetra, and is what is called the Kshetrajña the one who sees this world? Is that what you mean?

S.B. That is Kshetrajña. What one sees, that is Kshetra. In its pure meaning, Kshetra means the body. Kshetrajña means the Purusha within.

J.G.B. And he is the one who is enveloped in this consciousness?

S.B. Yes. He should forget this consciousness, and think of God. That means he is going beyond this consciousness.

J.G.B. But for the performance of duty, this consciousness is needed?

S.B. Yes, that is needed. For Meditation, consciousness is not wanted.

J.G.B. So this is the real secret—to use each power for the right purpose. For dealing with life, for duties, we need consciousness. For search for God, we need faith.

S.B. Reason also we require for consciousness.

J.G.B. But in a way, reason helps us in everything, even helps us to search for God, because by reason we know what we want.

S.B. No. There, what is needed is simple faith in God, not reason. There is a God—if I meditate on Him every day, I will see Him. This simple faith is all we need.

J.G.B. But isn't it my reason that tells me there must be God?

S.B. Reason says that there is something behind; but beyond that it cannot say more.

J.G.B. I understand—to go beyond this; to go to the belief that it is possible for me to have a direct connection with that Something, that is faith?

S.B. Yes.

J.G.B. Because reason will never tell that. And then, Babaji, how does faith arise in man? It is not then by experience that faith arises?

S.B. Because we see all these things existing. The question comes: What is this?

J.G.B. That is reason.

S.B. No. What is this: means it is beyond reason. We simply express our doubt. This is *this:* this is reason. That is *what:* this is not reason. When we say: I am a human being, it is reason. When we say: Who am I?, it is beyond reason. When we pursue this beyond reason, we reach God. When we pursue this reason, we reach pleasure.

J.G.B. This is how Death began to answer the Nachiketas' question. He said: There are two things; one is the pursuit of pleasure, the other is the pursuit of Truth, and the one leads this way, and the one leads that way. That is how he answered this question, isn't it?

S.B. These pleasures lead one to trouble indeed.

J.G.B. Yes, indeed. I thought that after all the refusals, Nachiketas says: I don't want this, I don't want that, then at last Death began to answer him in such a simple way.

S.B. When every temptation is rejected, Death begins to answer. Fear and temptation, these are the two beginnings of human troubles.

J.G.B. Fear comes from what we don't see, and temptation from what we do see. Between those two, we remain prisoners.

S.B. Yes. They turn us away from our real question; either fear or temptation will turn us away.

M.M. We hear very much about non-attachment, that we call identification. Is this the way out of fear and temptation?

S.B. Non-attachment must be from life only. Attachment for God there must be.

J.G.B. Yes, I remember last time I was here I said to you: must one put away even the desire for God, and you said: No, every desire must go, but not this desire for God.

S.B. But for everything else desire is an enemy.

J.G.B. Yes, and this desire for God must grow so strong that man will not be able to live without it. It must be stronger than desire for woman or for any other kind of satisfaction. It must be stronger than any natural desire. How to come to that strength is the question.

S.B. Go on; begin to live life like I tell you. It will automatically come.

J.G.B. I am sure that is true.

S.B. It will automatically come. There is a seed. The whole tree is in that seed. When the seed develops that tree comes. In the same way, when this life becomes more and more stable—that automatically comes. You see, human beings have no patience, they want everything in a hurry.

M.M. Yes; that's the trouble.

S.B. Yes. Yes, patience, even the whole oceans will be drowned within patience. It will come.

Yes, there is the story of a young boy Dhruva. His stepmother turned him out, he was very sensitive, he went to the forest. Then he sat under a tree, and he wanted to see God. Then a Saint going by said: 'You are very young, you won't get to God.' Then the boy said: 'No, no, don't say like that. Tell me where to see God.' The Saint said: 'I shall go and ask God and will give you his answer.'

So the Saint went to see God and told him what the boy was asking.

Then God said: 'I will not go to him, it will take a long time for me to go to him. He is sitting under a tree. Tell him to count the number of leaves in that tree. So many lives he should finish, then only will I go to him.' The Saint came back and told him: 'No use of your sitting here. So many lives you will have to pass, then only you will see God.' The boy said: 'All right, if I will pass all those lives, he will see me, that assurance he has given. I am satisfied.' He sat there. Then God wanted to test him. He took the form of a lion, and began to roar very fiercely, and He came near his side. The boy saw that lion, and then he said: 'Oh, Lion come up very soon and eat me away. One life is over. I am nearer God.' No fear, nothing in him. He wants only God; then at once, God revealed

73

Himself before him. This is determination. Fear should be driven out.

With all his insistence upon the need for an uncompromising determination in the pursuit of Truth, the Shivapuri Baba is well aware of the dangers of a literal interpretation. He told us a story that may not be so well known as the Nachiketas and Dhruva stories that are constantly quoted by Indian teachers and writers. This was told in reference to the tendency of people to leave their common-sense behind when they first embark on the search for spirituality.

S.B. There is an answer for each and every obstacle.

Once a snake was lying on the way. It used to bite everybody. A Yogi was passing. The snake went to bite him also. He (Yogi) said: 'No, there is sin, don't bite me.' He (the snake) said: 'What is sin?' The Yogi explained. The snake was frightened. 'What must I do?' said the snake. The Yogi said: 'Now, you don't bite anybody, keep quiet in your place, and take the Name of God.' He said this and went away. That snake remained in that place, and began to take the Name of God. Some children were passing by that way. They saw the snake. They took stones, and threw at it, and some mischievous children caught it by the tail, and threw it away. It was about to die. The Yogi was returning, then the snake called him. 'What a man you are. What you taught me? Now I am about to die. Why you taught me this nonsense?' The Yogi said: 'No, no. It is your own mistake. Why you remain in that particular place? Why did you not go and stay in your hole there? Nobody would have seen you. I told you not to bite people. When people come to trouble you, why do you not rear your head and frighten them? I told you not to bite them, that is all. They will run away. You could not use your intelligence, so that is why you came into trouble.'

In the same way when I ask you to practise discipline, some such mistakes will come. How that snake got the answer, if you will come to me at once you will get the answer. You can avoid that. So in the beginning a guide is most essential. It will be very good . . . for a developed intelligence, it is not so much. For others it is essential.

To end this attempt to convey what he means by Right Life,

I shall return to the notes provided by Thakur Lal Manandhar in August 25th, 1962.

"The other day two Germans heard me speak about Right Life and asked me, 'What is there in your Right Life that makes it superior to Christianity?' I said: 'Right Life is universal and Natural Life. Take breathing, for instance. Can you say: I won't breathe? So with eating, sleeping, thinking, feeling, etc. I say: Regulate these so as to keep your body all right, and your mind unperturbed. Then, to everybody naturally occur the questions: What is all this, this universe, this life, birth, death? What is the purpose of all this? What is at the bottom of all this? What is the goal of all these activities? Remain in these questions for as long as you can, remain longer and longer, you will know the Truth, and know and get something after knowing and getting, which no more will remain to be known or got, to attain which state is the natural desire of everybody in unclouded moments. Right Life asks us to remain in these natural desires and pursuits. This could be done and had been done even before any known teacher-propagated religion came into being, this was and is being done since the coming into being of all religions, and this will remain possible even after all these religions have gone into the limbo of oblivion. This is what makes it superior to Christianity, Vedic religion, etc. These religions came into being after mankind had vastly deteriorated, in order to provide some palliatives. But the final and only cure for all ills is Right Life alone. Vedic Religion is meant to awaken the dormant sense of the Natural Life. So also other religions serve this purpose in varying ways and degrees'."

The last extract is couched in the language of the Gita. The Swadharma of former times was outwardly fixed by the duties of caste, sex, age, etc. Nowadays, Swadharma has become something arbitrary that each one fancies he can know for himself. I have not changed the wording of the following passage. The approximate English equivalent of the few Sanskrit words are given in brackets. *S.B.* For all appearances the world is doing Swadharma alone. Because Swadharma means the protection of this 'I' and 'Mine', which everybody in the world has been following. But the only defect in them is that they are twisting this Swadharma to their own liking. Living according to teaching is real Swadharma, whereas living according to one's liking is Swartha-Dharma. This latter it is which the present world is doing. They are losing sight of knowledge and morality.

What is the most important object for us to attain to? This life, which we protect and cling to, is short and so not eternal. God is the most important object to be attained. Advaita philosophy does not attach importance to life and rushes headstrong to God-concentration, while Dvaita gives much importance to living this Swadharma and overlooks God. But both these attitudes are defective when taken singly. Both together constitute the truth. When the one is mentioned, the other is implied also. Without living Swadharma, God is an impossibility and, bereft of God, Swadharma has no meaning and loses its significance.

We are in this body and we must protect it in order to make ourselves able to peep towards God. Living Swadharma is nothing but the protection of this body and allied things. This is what the Gita means by Kshetra, and the necessity of Swadharma arose since we are confined to this Kshetra, meaning our body. Therefore we must conclude that Swadharma is something which is imposed on us. According to the Gita, the Self in us which looks after this Swadharma is Kshetrajña. But the real self in us, that is the Purusha (or Soul), is beyond all this limitation. It is Kshetrajña who has to seek his identity with the Purusha—our real self. But the trouble is that he is not allowed to achieve this until and unless his looking after this Kshetra is well attended to. This is why the necessity came for living Swadharma according to teaching.

When his work of living Swadharma is properly done, that is, with right knowledge and morality, no reactions are formed in him which tend to bind him down to earthly things, and so he is allowed quietly to sit for his other work, namely the higher one of seeking his identity with the Purusha. This Kshetrajña is only the imposed self of the Purusha. It is owing to our sin, or ignorance in another sense, that this real Purusha is hidden from our view. By perfectly establishing Swadharma, when this Kshetrajña will shake off his imposition and constantly concentrate on Purusha, he will

76

be able to realize his identity. The nature of this identity is what we call Sakshatkar or Realization.

At present, our attempts to concentrate our minds upon God; or, for that matter, upon any other object, recoil upon ourselves and we fail to make them our own. But once this 'identity' is achieved the situation is totally different. What is attained then, is ours forever.

There are opinions as regards this Meditation of God or Purusha. We can think and meditate on God as Saguna (with form) and as Nirguna (formless) both. Some advocate the one and others the other. Each party is wrong. Both together is the truth.

Whenever we think of anything we naturally form something in our imagination, and therefore we just begin with Saguna, but at the same time we are not losing sight of the fact that our object to be attained is verily without name and form. The one implies the other as the observe and reverse of the same coin.

Alluding to our subscription to *The Hindu*, a South Indian paper in English which we were then reading regularly and thinking of discontinuing, he said:

S.B. Previously we did not read newspapers. By chance we came to read some, and in course of time we liked it, and we even began to subscribe to it and have now become good readers. Now again we have no liking for it and have come to such a stage as to denounce it. So the case happens with all other things in this world.

From an unknown source comes something which we like for a time, and afterwards denounce it as something unwanted, and it disappears. When we begin to put up Swadharma we will not indulge in such extra things. We will do only what we have put up —only essentials. Please note that a man of Swadharma also can enjoy as a king, gain internal powers as a Siddha and at the same time remain in God-Contemplation, all on a much elaborate scale. This depends upon the standard and capacity of the man. If Swadharma is put up, he does not get lost in the details.

The Shivapuri Baba went on to explain the difference between Swadharma and Swartha Dharma, which means literally 'self-seeking'.

S.B. The difference is this, that while Swartha Dharma will leave

77

us in time as something quite unwanted or extra, Swadharma will last as long as we are here in this bondage of life. It is said that it follows us wherever we go, even in our lives to come. It is born with us, is living and will live with us in future too.

We are born in this world, we see this existence around. Naturally we begin to inquire: 'What is this All?, For persons who are capable of penetrating deeper, there is one higher Truth behind all this. They say: 'We must know That.' For incapable souls Veda comes forward, and declares that there is one Supreme God, and asks us to meditate on Him so that He may come and tell us the meaning of all this. This much is what has been spoken about this higher Truth. Veda, or any other teachings, cannot go beyond this in this respect, because speech comes back baffled and mind is powerless to penetrate. Thus goes the saying in the Upanishad: *yatoh vāchah nivartante aprāpya manasā saha* which means: 'That failing to reach Which, speech recoils along with mind.' From what is seen (that is, this existence), Veda begins to speak so as to introduce us to the things around us. It is therefore called Shruti, by the help of which we get ourselves acquainted with all the contents of this existence. Smriti is that which comes to let us know how to deal with this content, and Purana is that which comes to illustrate this dealing in the right manner. All scriptural teachings, if analysed, will come under these three main heads.

Now, while we go on inquiring as to what is there behind all these phenomena of existence or existence itself, we are drawn back by the call of the six senses. For instance, this hunger, thirst, etc., will draw our attention to the relative side, that is, this life. And we must come down and fulfil what the six senses need, or else we are not allowed to think on the Truth, which is behind, undisturbed. Thus two different lives came into being; one, the higher life—this contemplation on the Truth or God; the other, the lower life—this going to answer all the demands our life in this body makes upon us. We take to this lower life, that is, Swadharma, only to make the higher one possible. In the higher we have God, world and Purusha only. In the lower, Purusha, knowledge (or moral discipline), and intelligence (or physical discipline). The same Purusha comes down from the higher life and assumes so and so, and works with intelligence and mind. Therefore, the lower life consists of this assumed Purusha (or soul), knowledge (or mind), and intelligence (or action).

The higher life may be imagined to be like a point, while the lower one is its elaboration. For instance, when I say 'Take meals,' you will naturally go to gather materials and begin to cook. But the order is only to take meals. When I say 'Go to the top of this tree,' you will go only up to the point where you are safely upheld by the tree, not necessarily to the topmost point. There the trunk of the tree will break with its burden. The higher life is only a theory which we put into practice by leading the lower.

In all these talks the significance of Swadharma, or Right Life, takes shape and strength. It is, first and foremost, the exactly correct care of one's own body and its powers and functions. This Swadharma persists from birth to death, and is a condition of our liberation from the ties of earthly existence. The respect for the body implied in the Shivapuri Baba's exposition, is an echo of the Christian doctrine of the Resurrection of the body. Man is a complete being whose entirety includes and requires the physical body. The second aspect of Swadharma extends it to include one's own family and dependents. There is a Right Life which is not confined to one's own personal existence, but shared by the community of family life. This can be understood as the reflection of the cosmic order—the Universal Dharma—within the microcosmos of the human family. By our participation in this, we incur the obligation to preserve and also to fulfil the family Dharma. An obligation implies the ability to fulfil it. "Must implies can." We cannot fulfil our Dharma, either towards our own bodies or towards the family and society to which we belong, unless we have the means, *artha*. This word is commonly translated as wealth and it can be given a materialistic interpretation. But its true significance lies in the need for the means of action. Through the possession of *artha* we can do what is required of us. Therefore, the acquisition of wealth is a part of our duty. Evidently, this does not apply to the Sannyasin who has abandoned all possessions and with them all external activity; but even he must have the *artha* for fulfilling his primary duty of maintaining the body. Thus

79

it is that the Shivapuri Baba tells us that so long as he has breath he must continue to teach. At first, one might suppose that the highest and only right motive for teaching others would be their own welfare. But this would disregard the all-embracing character of Dharma. One's own Dharma must be fulfilled. What we do for the Dharma of others is part of the total Dharma, and it cannot be separated from our own.

Thus Right Living has three aspects; cosmic, social and personal. It is the Universal Law or Will of God. It is the principle of welfare of the human society. And it is also the individual destiny of each human soul. But the three aspects are inseparable. Dharma is one and indivisible.

I shall end this chapter by quoting answers he sent me by letter.

J.G.B. What is moral discipline?

S.B. If you want to know about moral discipline we will have to write a few volumes, but it is not possible now. You are a very intelligent man and so a few words in a nutshell can create the understanding of moral discipline in you. Mind's nature is to join with sentimentalism. If it is joined with sentimentalism it gets reacted in liking and disliking. This liking and disliking will prompt persons in going out of their ways and doing harmful things. Mind should join with reason. Then it will not get reacted in liking and disliking, and people will not go out of their ways and do unreasonable things. This is one explanation. Another explanation is when loss or gain, shame or fame, good or bad occurs, mind reacts and does unreasonable things. Mind should rise above these things and remain unperturbed irrespective of personal consequences and do the right thing. A third explanation is: Mind associates with lower nature and does irresponsible things. Mind should join with higher nature or virtues and behave properly. So higher nature is to be developed. Lower nature is to be curbed.

J.G.B. What is spiritual discipline?

S.B. Mind is filled with various impressions, passions and thoughts. All these should be emptied from the mind. God-thought alone should roam in the mind with one desire to see God or to have His blessings, or in other words, there is a Truth behind this life. That is to be known. The thought of this Truth alone should occupy the mind, no other thought.

By performing the three duties life will prosper but that will not create this moral and spiritual discipline. Moral discipline is to create peace in the mind. Without peace prosperity becomes meaningless. Meditation on God becomes impossible when there is no peace in the mind. When any desire remains, meditation is not possible. One's sole concern in life should be God-Realization. Life should become secondary.

My teaching is that one should know what is life, why is life and how is life. Without knowing these things life can never be lived properly. To know these things we should know God first. So one's aim should be to see God. To know God one should be possessed by that one idea of God exclusive of all other ideas. Therefore, one should always meditate on God. Now, in an impure mind meditation becomes impossible or distracted. For that moral discipline is essential. But again without a purified body, purification of mind also becomes impossible. To have a purified body one should do simple essential things. One should regulate all his duties and these regulated duties should be done with complete success. Hence disciplined actions.

Q. But the true worship is when I forget all forms and only surrender myself to God beyond name and form.

S.B. Surrendering our wills to God or forgetfulness of oneself. These are not the truth though it can be said so. When we think of God or meditate on Him there is a content in it. Let that content only be the object of your mind. That content will reveal the truth. No matter whether you surrender yourself or not, whether you forget yourself or not, the question is knowing this content. In Muhammedanism, in Christianity or in any other religion the content is the same. It is only expressed in various ways according to various conceptions.

Q. In this formless worship I have moments of intense bliss when it seems that I am aware of God. Is this the beginning of 'seeing God' to which you refer? Do you recommend any special form of meditation?

S.B. The bliss you experience in your moments of God-worship

81

should not be cared for. If you know this bliss you meditate on the bliss not on God. Therefore ignore this bliss and think only of God. I have asked you to do essential duties to live this life. You should have wisdom to avoid non-duties in order to do your duties successfully. I have asked you to practise virtues. You will have to practise them in order to make your mind *strong*. I have asked you to meditate on God. Here in this meditation you should exercise your own imagination. Do not follow anybody's teaching. How much you can spare every day so much should be utilized for meditation. There is no such special form of meditation to be recommended.

CHAPTER FOUR

THE THREE DISCIPLINES

THE reader who recalls the impact upon the President of India of the Shivapuri's doctrine of the Three Disciplines, will not be surprised to find an entire chapter devoted to this theme. When he first spoke of them to me, his words made a deep impression upon me; but I could not tell whether I was so affected by their content, or by the beauty of his presence and by the wonder of meeting one whom I could not but regard as a perfected human being. I assumed that his words had such power just because they were uttered by him. Later, as I came to reflect upon them, I saw that their power was not personal at all, but is due to their special relevance for the present-day world. Indeed, this is what he himself insisted. "It is not my person that matters," he said again and again, "but my teaching." In recommending me to write he said: "If you want your book to be useful to people, explain clearly and in full detail my teaching of the three disciplines, but leave my person out of it." This, as the reader will appreciate, is scarcely possible, but there is no doubt that the presentation of Right Life in terms of the three disciplines makes the notion accessible to people of all races, religions and cultures. In this respect, I would say that the Shivapuri Baba is more universal than any of the great Indian saints and sages of the last hundred years. This may be attributable to his forty years pilgrimage round the world, but it seems to me rather an indication of his greatness. I know of no other Asiatic teacher whose advice on the subject of man's earthly life can be applied with so little modification to the conditions of our Western civilization. This is the chief reason why I accepted the unexpected honour of being invited to write about his teachings.

In books by and about most of the great Indian teachers there are, of course, innumerable references to the duties of man, but the great majority refer to the varnāshrama, that is, to the four castes and the four states of life. Swami Vivekananda, in his lectures on Practical Yoga, classifies duties according to the three *gunas*, or qualities, *sattwa*, *rajas* and *tamas**, but this has no obvious connection with the three disciplines. Accounts of their personal dealings with hosts of men and women by saints and sages like Ramakrishna and Ramana Maharshi, Swami Ramdas and Ma Ananda Mayi, are to be found in their biographies and pilgrimage diaries; but I have not been able to find any exposition as realistic and practical as that given by the Shivapuri Baba.

I do not mean that he expounded any new principles or doctrines not to be found in the Hindu scriptures, or indeed in the *Bhāgavad Gita* alone. In a sense, his teaching could be called the 'Gita up-to-date', but it engenders a sense of novelty and wonder because of its power to penetrate beyond the screen of words and mental images. The following exposition is my own attempt—made on his express instructions—to state his teaching in terms familiar to Western Seekers of the Truth.

Man has a threefold structure, consisting of his body with its various functions and powers, his mind with its impulses, desires and qualities, and his will or spirit. Each of these three components has its own part to play in the life of man as a whole. The body is the seat of the Intelligence and the field of its activity. Thus the body is to be taken together with the various functions associated with it such as thought, feeling and sensation.

I have used the word mind as equivalent to the Sanskrit *Manas*, but it does not convey exactly what I understood him to mean. He often referred to the need for a 'strong mind' which can be acquired only by self-discipline. He also spoke of the mind as if it were a vessel that must not only be made strong, but also purified and put in good order. On the other hand, he never connected mind with thinking, as we should be inclined to do. I have been

* Other books I have examined include: Aurobindo *The Yoga and its Objects, The Gita Interpreted, The Mother*. Vivekananda *Lectures on the Three Practical Yogas Bhakti, Raja and Kama*. Swami Ramdas *The Pilgrimage* and *The Divine Life*. Ramana Maharshi's *Gospel*, Brahmananda *The Message of our Master*. Jean Herbert *Spiritualité Hindoue* and S. Radakrishnan *Introduction to Translation of the Gita*.

accustomed to use the word 'Being' for this part of man's nature, and to say that a man can have strong or weak being, pure or impure being, unified or divided being; and it seems to me that is what the Shivapuri Baba intended to convey by the word mind, which, by the way, he never confused with 'intelligence'.

The third part of man is called in Sanskrit the Purusha. I connect it with *Will*, which is the seat of the freedom given to man to choose between the different influences that act upon him, both from without and from the different sides of his own nature. I am sure that the Shivapuri Baba would agree that Purusha is the same as the Christian 'Spirit' of man, created directly by God and destined to return to its Source. The Purusha or self* is hidden behind the veil of our bodily experience, wrongly called 'consciousness', but really no more than organic sensitivity. For this reason, Purusha is helpless until the mind grows strong enough and wise enough to 'pierce the veil of consciousness'.

The three disciplines correspond to the destiny of the three parts of man's being. The Shivapuri Baba calls the three destinies: World-Realization, Soul-Realization and God-Realization. In studying Manandhar's notes, I observed with great interest that the Shivapuri Baba connects the three disciplines with, what he called in 1940, the 'basic elements', which are understanding, will and energy. This corresponds, if I have seized his meaning rightly, to the three parts of man's nature that I myself associate with being, will and function. He said that 'energy' comes from meals, sleep and the performance of one's duty. Life has many different functions all of which must be studied and performed under the first discipline.

The second discipline is that of the mind. This is the seat of the character, both good and bad. The mind must be both strong and pure. These are two opposite requirements and must be harmonized. Plenty of people have a strong but impure mind. They are able to dominate their own body and its energies, but

---

* The word Jiwa, or The Alive, is used as almost synonymous with Purusha or the Self. This is characteristic of a certain deliberate imprecision that is common in Eastern teaching. Viewed as that which is destined for liberation Jiwa is the same as Purusha, but viewed as the life-principle it is distinct. Again Jiwa may be the personal conscious mind which seeks Purusha.

they do so from mixed motives. Such people are unable to attain the serenity that is required for meditation. On the other hand, there are people whose mind is very pure, but it has not met with any great resistance, and overcome it, and therefore it remains weak. A weak mind, however pure it may be, will not be able to meditate successfully, for it will lack the necessary courage and persistence.

The direct way to acquire a strong and pure mind is by unswerving adherence to the virtues. By the practice of rejecting the harmful elements of one's own nature and embracing the good sides, the inner struggle is established by which the mind grows strong. This I would call *self-discipline* in the strict sense of the term.

Finally, there is the discipline of the will. This is attained solely by meditation. Here force is useless, for one cannot change one's own will by force. Over and over again in his talks, the Shivapuri Baba insisted upon the gratuitous character of the supreme good, that is, God-Realization. As in the story of the boy Dhruva, God reveals Himself to the Soul in His own good time and in His own manner. The soul is powerless here. Nevertheless, it has its own necessary part to play and that is to be single-minded in its waiting for God. This single-minded, patient waiting for God with loving insistence, is meditation. This is complete *worship*, that must be distinguished from devotion which is only one of the forms of worship.

We thus have the three primary divisions of Right Living; *Duty*, *Morality* and *Worship*. The guiding principle for *duty* is intelligence, for *morality* discrimination, and for *worship* spiritual longing. Of these three, he once said:

"The sole purpose of this human life is to find the Ultimate Truth or God, and for this we must accept a certain code of life which means that we should put our life in right order. There are three different orders we should look into. They are (1) Spiritual order; (2) Moral order; and (3) Intellectual order. At present we are wandering in disordered life. As long as we do not chalk out a mode of living, planned according to the three orders mentioned above, we can never hope to get out of this labyrinth of Saṁsāra."

86

The First Discipline of Duty: for a good life (Sukha) here on earth. This is not to be despised, for it is a condition that for most people must unavoidably be fulfilled if they are to go forward in the search for God. At first, it might seem that this is none other than Karma Yoga. But the point of Karma Yoga is to emphasize the need for non-attachment: action without desire for the fruits of action. The discipline of *duty* as explained by the Shivapuri Baba is essentially the right use of Intelligence. For the first discipline one must have a *keen intelligence.* Since he also said that the first duty is exclusively concerned with the body, one might connect it with Hatha Yoga, but this he dismissed as of minor significance, saying it was concerned either with health or the acquisition of special powers—the *siddhis*—which depend upon control of the material and psychic energies. It seems then that the first discipline does not fall exactly into any of the forms of yoga, but it is rather the fruit of the Shivapuri Baba's own meditations and experience of life in all parts of the world.

The first discipline falls into three parts, one is the immediate care of the physical body, another is the fulfilment of our social obligations, and there is also the duty to provide for ourselves and our dependents and to make right use of our powers and abilities. I have already quoted one or two descriptions of these duties, but will add another that he gave to Manandhar about twenty years ago.

"Since we have our bodies to maintain we have to perform duties.

"(1) *Personal:* To keep the body fit we have to use our external organs and we should use them wisely; that is, we should use them as much as is necessary. Seeing, hearing, speaking, touching, eating, etc., should be done only to the proportion required for the body and mind; no extra use should be made.

"(2) *Obligatory:* Since we cannot live alone and need the help of others, society is required. We have our duties to society, parents, family and other people.

"(3) *Professional:* Since we have to maintain ourselves, we must earn something and must take to some profession according to individual taste and capacity. But we should spend on our own

87

account only as much as is necessary and use the balance for other purposes. Spend what is absolutely necessary, nothing more, nothing less.

"These threefold duties are imperative for all individuals. They are ordained by God.

"We must establish our life first by performing these duties. Those who desire to realize the Truth should make the moral and physical disciplines of the three duties secondary, and the spiritual discipline, namely Meditation, primary. Those who like to enjoy life, should make the first discipline primary, and meditation secondary. But in no case should any of these duties be omitted. Life should be put in order and disciplined by performing the first three duties, each duty being performed strictly according to need. Whenever there is time after performing the first set of duties, one should concentrate on Meditation.

"These duties should be performed from childhood, that is during the period of Brahmacharya. One who is grown up, and who has not followed these duties previously, may also practise to perform these duties. There may be errors in the beginning, but, with a strong determination, a mature person may overcome the errors and defects, and order his life to lead a 'Right Life'.

"The success either in worldly life or in finding Truth is possible only by Swadharma. This life was practised in pre-Vedic days, when perfect order and harmony existed in the society without external force. When people forgot this life, Vedic teachings came and then came the Shāstras. Shāstras or Vedic teachings, and all annotations of Shāstras, like Sānkhya, Patanjali, Advaitabad, Dvaitabad, Visisthadvaitabad and all religious precepts, are all theories and they narrate or give only the partial truth. Only this Right Life and Meditation for Truth in a direct method lead to realization of the Absolute. Other Yogavyas—Karma, Jñana or Bhakti Yoga—or other practises of penance do not lead to realization of God. They only help to forget the miseries of life and bring happiness to the mind. All that comes from the performance of Yoga is *enjoyment* not *realization*.

"Just as a patient is chloroformed and is forgetful of the pain of the operation, so also the yogavyas make them forgetful of the threefold miseries of existence; they avoid the real problem of life and do not solve it. Death comes and takes away these people to the same place where they had been, and they are born again on this earth. They do not conquer Death, nor do they solve the problem of life—Realization of Truth. On the contrary, these yogas deteriorate Mind and Intelligence, and they lead people to more 'bhrams' or illusions."

This passage is characteristic of an original creative intelligence that can bring new influences into human life. In my experience I have found that such men invariably reject all other influences as useless or harmful and recommend strict adherence to their own advice. This does not mean that they are narrow or intolerant. None of the original teachers and spiritual leaders I have known personally were either the one or the other: the Shivapuri Baba least of all. But they have something of their own to say, and they will not dilute or adulterate it with other people's ideas. Yoga is the entire system of theory and practice which has been constructed upon the control of psychic energies. This system includes bodily energies such as those released by breathing exercises, emotional energies such as are given by devotional practices, mental energies obtained by various forms of concentration and the practice of much of what is called 'Meditation' or Samādhi. On the face of it, therefore, Yoga should provide a complete way of life culminating in the Beatific Vision in which the Yogin realizes his unity with God. The Shivapuri Baba seems to reject the claim that lies at the very heart of all Yoga and indeed of the Bhagavad Gita itself. But on reflection, one sees that what he rejects is the assumption that the Yogin achieves God-Realization by the power of his own unaided will.

I understand the Shivapuri Baba to mean that none of these exercises, nor any combination of them, will lead to Knowledge of God. They may lead to various blissful experiences, and even to a permanent state of detachment and rapture, but this is not God-Realization. Nor can they even be regarded as sound means for preparing the soul for the final step, unless they are combined with, and subordinate to, a strictly disciplined life. All is useless and a waste of time unless God chooses to reveal Himself to the soul.

This, the Shivapuri Baba makes very clear in another statement recorded by Manandhar. He says:

"There is a sharp and material distinction between the stage of going beyond consciousness and the stage of senseless stupor, which in other words is called 'Nirvikalpa Samādhi'. 'Nirvikalpa Samādhi' is a state of happiness—a kind of enjoyment. It creates a vacuum in the Mind which becomes forgetful of the worries of the world. It gives a mental bliss, but no knowledge nor any wisdom. It merely negates the world and with it the 'I'—the Knower—who will realize the Truth. Nirvikalpa Samādhi is no doubt a very high stage of Yogasādhanā, but it is limited by the lack of Knowledge of the Absolute. In direct Meditation, when the knower goes beyond consciousness, he is oblivious of the external world but not of the internal world, nor of the positive journey he is constantly making towards the Absolute. He is unconscious so far as his external senses are concerned, but he must be fully conscious of himself, of the Soul and its relation with God. By this he goes beyond Māyā (i.e. appearances both sensory and mental) and goes straight to God. Nirvikalpa Samādhi takes one to the border line of Māyā, but not beyond. By simple denial of the senses it does not help to go beyond Māyā and to know the Truth. Right life and Meditation, on the other hand, takes one beyond Māyā and to **Truth**."

The Shivapuri Baba does not assert that the duties of life are obligatory for every soul. Those who have exceptional strength and purity of mind can go forward direct to the search for God. But this is not a way that the ordinary man can follow, and many have come to grief by trying to do so. In one of his talks with Manandhar in 1937, he said: "Some people by nature are easily disturbed by such unfavourable happenings in the external world, that is, in life. To such weak people, this adjustment to the external world is of utmost significance and, therefore, compulsory. But there are exceptional cases everywhere. There are strong souls, like Buddha, Ramakrishna, Ramana Maharshi, who can ignore this disturbance, and at the same time maintain keeping their full attention upon God. They are strong enough to resist pain or temptation in the external and worries in the internal world. To such people this work of perfecting Knowledge and Intellect is not of so much importance, and can be made optional and not compulsory. But this exception is not advisable for all. This compulsoriness varies according to the resisting or ignoring capacity of the man in question. To that extent every one must look to it. But, as a rule, both are to be prescribed, that is, God plus life-adjustment. This is the royal road as prescribed by the Gita. But as a short cut for the man in question, this importance attributed to Knowledge and Intellect may be disregarded, according to his capacity for resisting or ignoring the reactions produced by wrong Knowledge and wrong Intellect. But beware of strong reactions."

The First Discipline—Bodily

The foundation of the first discipline is *Discrimination*. In his talks with me, he referred to this as the fruit of a keen intellect rightly used. A man was sitting by him and was offered a cigarette. He did not smoke, so he took a few puffs out of courtesy. Then he looked for a place to throw his cigarette. The earth was swept so clean that there was not even dust to be seen. The flower beds were so beautifully kept that to throw a cigarette among them would have been sacrilege. Not wanting to get up and lose what the saint was saying, he chose a moment to ask what he should do with the cigarette butt. The Shivapuri Baba smiled benignantly and said: "That is discrimination. Other people come here and throw their cigarettes on the earth without seeing how it is kept clean: but you have used your eyes and your intelligence. That shows that you have discrimination."

He also insisted upon the importance of careful attention to detail. I have given the examples of Manandhar's flower-buying and the art of tea-making, but he also referred to knowledge of one's own body. It is an obligation for man to study the peculiarities of his own body so as to know exactly how it should be treated. This is part of a normal education—Brahmacharya—but if neglected in youth such neglect can be remedied. Only one must never become interested in the body as such. One should know it as one knows an instrument that one has to make use of every day. The inner working parts of the instrument are just as important as its outward appearance. The body is the source of energy for all our activities. It must be looked upon in this way. We are not concerned with the likes and dislikes of a motor, but with its efficiency in giving the energy we need. It should be the same with the body. Of this he once said:

"For all this, there should be a regular routine of life. Meals, sleep and bath should be taken in exactly the right amount."

Of the 'science of sleep', he said, At every stage of life one must know exactly when to sleep, how long to sleep and how to sleep. If this is not known the body cannot be preserved. He continued: Life has many different functions. Prepare a regular time-table for each function. Regularity and punctuality in our daily routine is necessary. Each function is governed by a certain law. A practical application of the twenty-six qualities in each function brings one to the realization of the law of life. The fixed duties or functions should bind one according to the time-table made. No extra duties other than these should steal away one's energy, one's vital forces. All the different functions as a whole should tend towards the ultimate goal. They are like motives tending towards the Master Motif which is our ultimate goal. By daily observation, we come to know where the functions have been going wrong and improve our efficiency, till a time comes when we get a definite standard of life. We shall then have no inferiority in anything.

Observe cleanliness. Bedding should be neat and clean. No agitation, nothing should disturb when going to bed. Do not give way to speculation. Have calmness and concentrate on OM. Burn incense for good smelling.

Once the routine of the bodily life is well established we should pay attention to the other matters.

For the Western visitor, these were described as: family and social duties, professional duties, and the four charities. These latter are:

Think only good thoughts of others.

Speak only good words of others.

Do only good deeds to others.

Give of your substance to help others.

For the Hindu disciple, they are connected with the Gita: Yajna, Dāna and Tapas, or sacrifice, charity and self-control.

Yajnas are of five kinds viz. Brahma Yajna, Rishi Yajna, Pitri Yajna, Bhūta Yajna and Manushya Yajna.

Brahma Yajna—Early rising at Brahma muhoorta, ablutions (snana), Meditation (dhyana), study of scriptures, holy pilgrimage, fasting etc. Bath to be taken as prescribed. Meditation upon a single idea. Worship of an idol. Study of scriptures. Pilgrimage according to Sattwic ideal. Observing fast periodically. All such practices come under this Yajna. One should study from gods their specific qualities or virtues. This kind of activity is meant to cultivate a sense of responsibility and vigilance. With reverence and love or a Sattwic temperament always, we should have a keen sense of responsibility and vigilance so that we can avoid failures.

Rishi Yajna—Service to the teacher and holy association (Satsanga and Guru Seva). In this kind of activity, the qualities expected come forth automatically by the grace of the Guru (or teacher), since he points out our defects and brings inspiration to cultivate a Sattwic temperament. Real knowledge comes from this particular activity to achieve a higher realization of our being.

Pitri Yajna—Sacrificing something for our deceased ancestors with a sense of gratefulness for what they had done for us. This part of activity is to cultivate a sense of gratefulness and regard.

Bhūta Yajna—Feeding a cow, a dog or any other animal and birds. We sacrifice something for them. We show sympathy and kindness or love in our dealings with them. Their specific qualities should be appreciated.

Manushya Yajna—Sacrificing for our fellow beings, such as helping our friends, hospitality, daily feeding a friend or a relative or a poor man (helping the needy). This kind of activity is of immediate help to us. Our circumstantial difficulties can be greatly reduced as a return.

Tapas is lawful activity—Severe austerity in sticking to our plan of action at any risk. Forbearance and humility in our dealings with others are the qualities to be developed under this head. Tapas is of two kinds; one subtle and the other gross:

(1) Through mind—Checking the mind when it wants to go out-

side our appointed course of duties, retaining its normal state and not being influenced by emotions, agitations, etc. due to passion, wrath, greed, ignorance, etc.

(2) Through wisdom—to be aware of evil counsel which brings failure, to see which of the twenty-six qualities are lacking in the wisdom applied.

To sum up: the five yajnas are for peace (or Shanti). This is the business of the Soul.

(1) Brahma yajna brings sense of responsibility and vigilance.

(2) Rishi yajna brings inspiration and cultivation of all the 26 qualities.

(3) Pitri yajna brings gratefulness and regard.

(4) Bhūta Yajna brings sympathy and love.

(5) Manushya yajna brings love and fellow feeling.

Dāna is of four kinds, viz. Through mind, word and deed and by wealth. Good thought—through Mind. Sweet, short and true speech—through sound or word. Expression of the same in our actions. Tapas brings wisdom to follow virtuously a fixed programme of life.

The Second Discipline—Morality

In some of the earlier explanations, the first and second disciplines are combined. When he spoke to us in the last years of his life, the distinction between them was emphasized, even to the extent of asserting that the discipline of body of itself does nothing for the mind, and the discipline of mind of itself does not take care of the body. I was much impressed by this distinction, which corresponds to the conclusions I had reached as a result of forty years' study of human psychology according to the ideas and methods of Gurdjieff. Duty is the regulation of our functions and their powers, in accordance with the requirements of life on the earth. It can generally be expressed in the form of commandments such as are found in great detail in ancient scriptures, like the Code of Hammurabi, the Pentateuch, the Vedas and Brahmanas. With duty, one knows where one is. The Shivapuri Baba, however, added the important rider that Swadharma requires more than general rules of conduct; it calls also for an intelligent appreciation of one's own powers and limitations and the conditions of life in which we find ourselves. Duty with him becomes an exact science to be studied by observation, experiment, prediction and verification.

The requirements of that part of man which he calls the Mind are entirely different. Manas is the seat of strength, and it would perhaps be better translated as heart than mind. This is confirmed by the association of Manas with the emotional character rather than with the intellectual activity.

I have kept the word 'mind' chiefly because I can still hear the reverberation of his voice saying: "You must have a *strong* mind," with the letter O pronounced as no Englishman could, a long, deep vowel. Although a 'stout heart' perhaps renders the meaning better, it would not do here.

The strong mind is the link between the two worlds in which man has to live. It enables him, on the one hand, to face his duties with serenity; and, on the other, to enter upon his search for God with peace and faith.

The mind is thus the link between the spiritual and the material sides of man's nature, and also between the inner and the outer worlds in which we must live. In order to fulfil its task, the mind must be strong enough to withstand the assaults and pressures of the material world, and yet pure enough to recognize the delicate and subtle qualities of the spirit.

The transformation of the mind is thus the central problem for those of us, and they are almost the totality of all human beings on earth, who were not born, like Ramana Maharshi, with a mind strong enough and pure enough to embark without preparation or training upon the spiritual quest.

To the question: "How does one acquire a strong mind?" he gave the simple answer: "By the practice of virtue." A more detailed explanation is taken from the sixteenth chapter of the Gita entitled "Discrimination between the Divine and Demonic Endowments." The opening verses of this chapter enumerate twenty-six 'divine endowments' (Sampadam daivim). These are: Fearlessness, Purity of Mind, Stability of Character, Charitableness,

Self-Mastery, Readiness to make Sacrifices, Studiousness, Ability to make Efforts, Straightforwardness, Non-Violence, Truthfulness, Freedom from Wrath, Renunciation (of the fruits of action), Tranquillity, Aversion to Slander, Compassion towards Living Beings, Non-Covetousness, Gentleness, Sense of Shame in doing evil actions, Strength of Mind, Energy, Forgiveness, Endurance, Chastity, Absence of Malice, Aversion to Praise. The demonic endowments are the opposite of these. Only six of them are specified: ostentation, arrogance, excessive pride, anger, hardness of heart and ignorance.

Now all these qualities or endowments (sampadam) seem to be simple enough; they are just good or bad traits of character. This is faulty psychology and is clearly not intended by the words of the Gita. The sampadams are either daivic or asuric, that is to say, they come either from a divine or from a demonic source. They are not a part of the man himself, but influences that seek to act upon him, and between which he must choose.

This the Shivapuri Baba makes clear by saying that they are the *contents of the mind*. They are not attributes of the man himself, the *Purusha*, who is within or behind the mind. If he says: "I am truthful," or "I am angry or hard or ignorant," he should be careful to recognize that the copula 'am' does not refer to his being, but to his inclination towards the attribute in question. If one says "I give way to anger," it is both psychologically more accurate and also more in accordance with the text of the Gita. If we identify ourselves with the divine attributes, we fall into the sin described in Gita 16.15: "I am nice and well-born. Who is like me? I will offer sacrifices. I will give gifts. I will have bliss." Thus they speak deluded by ignorance. This is, of course, the same sin as that of the Pharisee who lifted his eyes to heaven and thanked God that he was not as other men are (Luke 18. 11).

We may then conclude that the Shivapuri Baba intends us to take him literally when he says that the higher and lower natures are the *contents of the mind*. What then is the mind that it can be a container of contents? It is evidently like a vessel into which we can pour good wine or bad, or like the field in which both wheat and tares can grow. The similes are helpful to emphasize the externality of the mind. It is not the person, the Purusha, the true man within, nor even the Jiwa seeking liberation.

We must, however, add the further notion that the mind itself is a living, sensitive and even conscious organ. As such, it is capable of undergoing transformation. This transformation comprises three distinct actions:

(1) The Mind must be purified, so that its contents consist wholly and solely of the daivic elements. This is a sattwic mind.

(2) It must be strengthened and expanded, so that it can withstand the influences of the external world and give the Purusha a place for tranquil meditation. These are serenity and peace.

(3) It must commit itself wholly and irrevocably to the search for God. For this, it must lose itself. This self-losing is described by the Shivapuri Baba as piercing the veil of consciousness. Only a strong, pure and wise mind can permit the act of renunciation. And yet it is not the mind itself that makes the act. This must come from the will, that is the Purusha within.

The transformation of the mind is a process distinct from the fulfilment of duties. The latter is the condition of spiritual progress, but the former is the direct means whereby it is achieved. This is the second discipline which the Shivapuri Baba characterizes as *moral*.

Morality is *sattwa*, that is purity, and right intelligence is *karma*, that is right action. The rajas and tamas gunas are connected with the demonic influences in the mind, and so, likewise, are useless (akarma) and harmful (vikarma) actions.

The difference between morality and duty is that the former concerns the inner life and the latter the outer life. The moral problem concerns exclusively the inner content. Actions in themselves cannot be described as moral or immoral unless we know the inner state from which they proceed. The Shivapuri Baba, in a talk with Thakur Lal, during the last world war, said that the conflict of duties need not mean a conflict of moral principles. In principle, morality means remaining in the *sattwaguna* and *karma* only, but situations may arise when this fixed rule ceases to be applicable. He said:

"Try to remain always in Sattwa guna and karma only. But

according to time, place and circumstances we shall have to come down either to Rajo guna or Tamo guna, not spoiling all the while our Santosh or serenity. In the case of intellect as well, sometimes we will have to do akarma and vikarma also according to time, place and circumstances, maintaining at the same time the resultant *Sukha* unhampered. In the case of morality also the same attitude is to be kept. Take as example, your action in coming here to me instead of going to Gokarna as ordered by your grandfather. Morality is not maintained. You incur the risk that he will learn of your failure to obey him and this will lead to disturbing happenings. There is no peace within. Nevertheless, this very same breach of morality can be made to serve for your own advantage. Thus you lose *Shanti* and you gain *Satsang*.

"We try to go beyond the gunas, but for all practical purposes we must have a foothold on one of them. For that, Sattwa is to be chosen always. Here too we can come down to Rajas or Tamas according to the demand made to us in relation to time, place and circumstances. We do so for our own advantage for the time being. This we can do for the preservation or protection of this 'I' and 'Mine'.

"Thus sometimes we can do akarma and vikarma as well when forced by a higher will or when one's interest of 'I' and 'Mine' is at stake. Example: celebrating my birthday with a feast. The work itself is akarma or useless and harmful as well in as much as we lose our time, money, etc. But in case we fail to do it, there is another bigger loss in the shape of losing my friendship and good-will. This is what you had in mind. So a small loss can be accepted in order to protect you from a greater loss.

"Stealing is akarma and vikarma also, but when a man steals a portion from a miser's hoard, leaving something for him to maintain himself, and distributes the rest among the destitute; in this case he has used discrimination to protect many by robbing one. Like this, right discrimination is at the root of all this bending. This flexibility in attitude is permissible only to a man of discrimination.

"Sin or no sin is not the question for a discriminative mind. A hangman is not responsible for the murder of a criminal. His soul, mind and intellect remains as pure as before. But the nature of his work is tamasic and yet he is quite prepared for it. He is not in the least affected in his Sukha, Santosh and Shanti—Well-being, Serenity and Peace. So we must be when we are forced to retreat or come down to lower gunas, lower works and breaches of morality. A hypocrite is disturbed in Sukha, Santosh and Shanti, whereas a man of discrimination is not at all disturbed, though to all appearances he seems to be a first-class hypocrite."

Here a very important property of the mind is brought to light, namely discrimination and flexibility. The moral discipline is of little use if it makes the mind rigid and unresponsive to the infinite variety of situations that it will have to meet in its pilgrimage towards Truth. The following beautiful little sermon illustrates the need for discrimination:

"In normal times we generally live our lives quite happily, giving as much attention as is necessary to our daily run of duties.We have our fixed principles and fixed ideas, and with them we keep up our balance of mind. We are not disturbed by anything whatsoever, and so we go on smoothly with our normal course, with the result that peace and happiness is ever flowing in our mind. As long as we are following our ordinary course of living, we never expect any change in our circumstances that might disturb our mental equipoise.

"But no. It is simply our blindness to World-nature. Anything may happen to us at any time quite unexpectedly. Abnormal circumstances come to us at times and we are thrown out from our seats. We become helpless and have to succumb to such overwhelming force from the external. The result is that our peace of mind is disturbed and so we lose our previous position. All our structures in the form of routines and principles tumble down and we are thrown into a state which is quite new and foreign to us. What happens? We generally get stupified and cannot easily recover our mental balance. We become like a fish out of water and we get lost in the whirlpool of Saṁsāra. What do we do? We try to regain our previous position, thinking that this is the only course left open to us in order to preserve that peace of mind we were enjoying previously. Here, we are mistaken. We overlook the fact

99

that our effort to regain our previous status is quite futile because in this ever-changing world what has happened will never return. Instead, if we are wise we should try to adjust ourselves to the new status in which we find ourselves. New schemes and projects we must introduce which are adaptable to the present conditions and build anew. To look back and bemoan the loss of our previous status is death to us. We should know that this change in circumstance is due either to some external happening or force; or else to our own indulgence or choice, that is, of our own making.

"In our past status, we had our fixed items of duties, and upon that structure or basis we were preserving our mental equilibrium. Now the situation demands their complete overthrow and we have to begin anew. We have not learned to change. The reason, if we pry deep, reveals itself as the incapability of our mind to fluctuate. When we make rules or fix our appointments, our mind follows them. But if there is a blind following, the mind is said to have no flexibility or capability to change. If there is illumination in those fixed laws, that is, if they have life, they must accept the change. It therefore follows that there is no law which does not admit of change. Everywhere there are exceptions to every rule. Our Hindu system of laws admits of exceptions because of this truth of the changing universe. This peculiarity of our Hindu law has become a target of criticism in the West, simply because it always admits of fluctuation. When a work is given, we generally do it according to a law prescribed, but this law is open to change with the changing circumstances. The peace and happiness that we get as the result of doing our duties is the Truth. Only if there is illumination on the part of the doer in connection with the law, so that he can recognize how the law permits change, and if his mind is quite prepared to change with the changing circumstances, can the Truth be realized in full. This is what we call *Karma kaushala* or dexterity in action."

At this point some questions were put to the saint. The first concerned the distinction between three Sanskrit words commonly translated as 'mind'.

S.B. *Manas, Buddhi* and *Ahamkāra* are all mind. Manas does,

Buddhi knows and Ahamkāra ascertains. A strong mind is possible through practice of the virtues.

Q. How does the mind do rightly?

S.B. When mind is impure, an action is done and there are pain and pleasure, love and hatred. When an action is done for its own sake, mind is said to act through reason.

Q. Will reading the scriptures help us to fill our mind with the right qualities?

S.B. Study of the Bhāgavat is for cultivating devotion to God.

Study of the Ramayana is for cultivating morality.

Study of the Mahābhārata is for cultivating dexterous intellect.

It must never be forgotten that the mind occupies a position that is necessarily ambiguous. It is turned out to the world and it is turned in towards the self. It must act and yet not be involved in action. It must know and yet not rely upon knowledge. It must cultivate morality and yet not imagine that morality alone will open the door that leads to God. This ambiguity is very characteristic of Indian spirituality, and is by no means confined to the Shivapuri Baba. Jean Herbert, in his book on Hindu spirituality, refers to the many ways in which this ambiguity pervades Indian thought. It is derived from a deep sense of the incompatibility of the infinite (Brahman) and the finite (Māyā), which cannot be resolved by refusal to face the problem. However much we may say Brahman alone is real, Māyā remains obstinately present to our senses and also to our mind. The Purusha may be concerned only with the Infinite to which it belongs, but mind must reckon with the power of Māyā to disturb the tranquillity of the inner self. Here I can quote directly from one of the talks given by the Shivapuri Baba in the early days of Manandhar's association with him, some time round 1948.

A right dealing with this Māyā is to be known and practised. This existence (that is what we see or this universe) is Māyā, with which we must have a right kind of dealing. We should have this unified idea that each and every part of what we see has God within itself. So everything is God. With this attitude (or Bhāvanā) we keep the right morality. For instance, if we have this kind of attitude we will not defile a girl or any other thing. This feeling of sacredness is what we should have in this right dealing. Next, the nature of what we see must be known. For instance, when we know the nature of fire we would not touch it with our hands, but would use tongs instead. Right morality (that is with no liking or disliking) is the tongs with which we should deal with this existence. We must do only as we are ordained. Lastly, we feel the effect that this Māyā creates what we call re-actions. We will neutralize them by dexterous action. When useless or harmful actions are not done, no reactions come to us. We then are left free to meditate upon God. Thus the Higher Life is made possible.

Like young boys playing with toys, you are now playing with life. You have not yet taken on the responsibility of a grown-up man. You are running after worldly pleasures and pursuits. You are satisfied with what little joys and sorrows come out of it. You have indulged in the pleasures of life so much that you have lost your sensitivity to what life really is. Now stop your tendency towards the pleasures of life and think. You will find that life is a mystery. You cannot know how and why it came into being.

Now let its existence be granted. Let us see its real aspects. It is a very important thing, more important than your near and dear ones, your personal hobbies and ambitions. It is a dear possession, dearer than your wife and children. It has no price. Even priceless jewels amounting to all the wealth of the world cannot compensate for its loss. We love this and cannot stop pouring our heartiest blessings for having got it.

But at the same time, if we look to the other side of it, we discover that life is a curse, a wretched thing, the vilest bondage. Look what troubles and sufferings we have to undergo as our obligations to it. Imagine a he-ass following a she-ass with joyful and amorous feelings, but getting in return kick after kick, and yet he persists. In like manner, you are running after life. Hunger and thirst, together with their concomitants, and, above all, our utmost anxiety to retain possession of life itself, are forcibly imposed on us. If you are a self-respecting man, you would not follow in its wake, when you come to realize that you only get kick upon kick from it. You will ask yourself: why should I care for it at all. These are the twofold aspects of life, which show that there is inconsistency in life.

The task of mind is to face this inconsistency and give to each side its due, to render unto Caesar the things that are Caesar's and unto God the things that are God's. The foundation of true morality, as distinct from artificial or imitative morality, is discrimination. This is the second and most precious possession that man can have—the first is insatiable hunger for Truth, that is God. Discrimination is an active power that goes beyond knowledge. We cannot discriminate rightly and act wrongly. If we see what has to be done and do not do it, we must admit that we do not discriminate.

Discrimination is a property of the mind—or, as we should say in the West, of the soul—which determines our actions. True discrimination is true morality. Morality without discrimination can always fall into error.

This interpretation of the Shivapuri Baba's teaching on Discrimination and Mind is confirmed by the following conversation that took place between him and my wife Elizabeth in 1961.

E.B. We live in an age that lacks faith. What can I do to bring my children up to have faith in a world that does not believe?

S.B. You cannot teach Faith. Faith comes from God. You must teach them discrimination. From discrimination, faith will come by itself.

E.B. How can they acquire discrimination?

S.B. By self-discipline. As soon as they reach the age when they can understand what you tell them, you must give them duties in the house. They must accept these duties and fulfil them without commission or omission. From this they will learn to observe and to eliminate. This is the way to acquire discrimination.

Then you must help them by showing them when they have done rightly, and when they have done wrongly. This is not to be done by praise and blame, which do not develop discrimination, nor by reward and punishment which destroy it. For example, you must never say: 'If you do such and such a duty well, I will reward you.' They must learn to perform actions for their own sake not for their reward. If you wish to reward them, you must do it afterwards, without their expectation of any reward. Then it will help them.

If you will follow these practices and show them how to cultivate the virtues, they will acquire discrimination automatically. Then Faith will be given them by God as soon as they are ready to receive it.

Manandhar also reports another conversation that connects the development of mind and discrimination with the upbringing of children.

S.B. At present you are living like pigmies when the state of your intellect and mind are considered. Your mind is quite under-developed, and so is your intellect. To make the idea clear, you should see the growth of a child's mind. It likes one thing but dislikes another, although the latter may be equally wholesome to it as the former. Here, its mind has taken to likes and dis-likes with no reason at all. To grow beyond this little mind, it should live on and grow in the company of its family members; then, in the long run, it will come to know that the thing it dis-liked previously is a thing now to be loved. It has thus to outgrow its past indiscriminate partiality. By living with the surrounding people and seeing their actions and habits, he gradually gains some more ideas. Mind's vision gets more and more enlarged, and the result we see is that the thing which it disliked at first, is now loved and endeared. Another illustration: when somebody calls, the child fears to approach him. It is because he is an unacquainted fellow. It has no scruples to approach its own people who have become quite familiar. This is due to the smallness of its intellect. It cannot know and appreciate the man who calls it. Intellect has not sufficiently grown to know the man with whom it should establish its friendship. Thus do we find the deficiencies in our intellect as well as our mind. To make up for this deficiency, we should have sufficient mental and spiritual growth.

How to grow is a question which always confronts us. As in the case of the child alluded to, we ought to live in the company of yogis or developed souls, and, by seeing and hearing their dis-courses, scriptural sayings and injunctions, we can in time develop our low mental states. By way of Shravana, manana, etc., that is by hearing and taking interest in knowledge, we can in time develop our intellectual capacity also. So to be a full-fledged being, we require mental growth as well as intellectual, and one without the other is not the truth. Both should grow side by side. For example, in the present-day world we find only intellectual growth to some extent, whereas there is no high moral principle guiding the people. Mental growth is pitiably overlooked. To define more clearly, the function of our intellect is to give light. For an officer, it is the intellect that defines and gives him an idea of the duties and functions of his office. That is, the intellect in him comprehends the laws, rules and regulations pertaining to his duties as an officer. But as the mind in him is not fully grown, and consequently no moral principles are being kept up, he does not hesitate to take bribes. His mind cannot stand the temptation and so he cannot carry out his duties successfully. He fulfils his duties in letter but not in spirit. So intellectual growth alone cannot shine without moral principles or sufficient mental growth. Mind is so weak that it cannot shake off the degrading influence of the three gunas or low mental states. Their names are Sattwa, Rajas and Tamas while their forms are Ichchhā, Rāga and Dwesha; that is, Longing, Passion and Hatred. Intellect wants something to be done but mind, under the influence of Longing, Passion and Hatred, does quite another. This is where our human weakness lies. How to grow beyond?

Here, we require saints and prophets and scriptural study. By living in their association, and by doing works of charity and virtues, we gain and grow. Likewise, mental or moral growth without intellectual upbringing cannot shine. They are so interrelated that one without the other has no beauty. Only after having achieved the two growths, can the man be said to have taken the right turn. He is then quite happy. His soul becomes free to look after its own welfare, as a mother gets free to indulge in her day's work, when her children come of age and are grown up enough to shoulder their responsibilities themselves. The soul's burden is unloaded and it is left at ease. We then become capable souls able to give way to our spiritual growth. Thus, side by side with the growth of mind and intellect, we are stepping on to divine heights.

How far the lower is achieved, so far also the higher life is made available.

From Manandhar's notes, it is clear that the distinction between the discipline of intelligence and the discipline of mind, between duty and moral perfection, developed gradually in the course of twenty years as more and more people began to come to the Shivapuri Baba to be shown the way of life. This does not mean that the distinction of body and mind was not always present; but, at first, in his explanations, the discipline of the practice of virtue was combined with the discipline of duty. The following extract from one of the earliest talks, in 1937, will show how he taught at that time.

"After a time, when a regular speed is gained in working out one's routine of duties, the virtues should be taken out for practice one by one in order. When this speed is gained the first part of the struggle is over and the virtues are further posts to be gained in like manner. Obstacles or difficulties may come, but we should never yield, even at the cost of our own life.

"Keep a tug of war with our mind always. When we do not yield, we drag the mind with greater force. But the mind will not retreat soon. It will be defeated only gradually in course of time. We should only go on with our duties. The question of time only remains. The day is sure to come. Now in the early stages we should take refuge in our routine, sticking to it at any cost. In course of time we will come to a stage when we can discard all undesirable or useless activities, and get ourselves refined. We shall have refined wisdom, with which we shall gain further posts. Our beginning is therefore a systematic or scientific process of refining our wisdom. Stick to one's principles, never change your principle for the whole life.

"We cannot get wisdom directly. Virtues are the stepping stones to it. What is virtue? A proper functioning of our daily routine of duties—Nitya and Naimittika. Living strictly according to the law governing these two is virtue in its real sense, which means a serious and strenuous sticking to duties. Going against the law, or taking light of the duties, or failure to work on the daily routine is Vice.

"Our activities should be real. Do not think in terms of good and bad. Think only in terms of what is real. A real action is produced by two forces—one is the commanding power, and the other is the controlling power. The so-called great men of the world have good commanding power in more or less degree. But when you critically analyse their actions, you will find that they do not have the controlling power. Their actions are either good or bad. By their way of self-discipline they have earned the commanding power to an extraordinary extent, but they have failed miserably in controlling that power so that they do not gain a real success in life. With the commanding power, they possess more than sufficient materials at their command, but they fail to know how to adjust or control the materials according to their requirements. To concentrate one's commanding power to a necessary extent, and use it, is a power possessed by a very few and exceptionally rare people. To gain reality, one should, according to one's circumstances in life, acquire the controlling as well as the commanding power.

"In our particular case, we must have a real command over our internal forces, and control them when we do our particular activities. Our sticking to the daily routine, with fixed duties, fixed time and fixed principles, means that we acquire this commanding power. But with this alone we do not get real success. We need that power only to the extent necessary for our particular ideal and use it. When we shall be able first to command our forces with fixed duties, fixed time and fixed principles, we shall have to control this power. The application of the twenty-six endowments, which are our higher nature, aims at controlling this power."

It must never be forgotten that mind should be the servant of the self and not the master. It acquires a power of independent action partly as a result of our own nature, and partly from our ignorance and bad associations. When the mind is in this state, the *Ahamkāra*, which should be searching for the self, searches only for satisfaction. This is the state of egoism from which the mind must at all costs be purified and delivered. Hence the Shivapuri Baba speaks of 'subduing' the mind: "A man under the influence of mind is a very weak soul. If this mind is subdued, God is very near. Do not allow anything from the external to make you desist or refrain from your duties.

"When there is disease in the body we lose our joy of life—no taste, etc. So also when there is ignorance our Purusha is unhappy. Make hay while the sun shines. Before nightfall we should reach our destination. Make haste. Speed up. Throw off idleness, slow-going and the like. You have determined, yes, but still mind is unwilling. This unwillingness is to be rooted out slowly, by degrees, because this sort of mentality is difficult to be driven out immediately. Only when we give way to virtues this will slowly vanish. This place is now occupied by you and so, without your leaving it, no other body can occupy it. In like manner this—your previous mentality—is taking hold of you. Slowly, by the practice of charity and virtues, this mentality will vanish out of sight. Like your child, this mentality is now under growth, and at present you have somehow to yield to its obstinacies. When it will come of age, you will then have to deal with it roughly even, i.e., you will have to refuse your support."

The Third Discipline—The Spiritual Life

We now reach the supreme task, the fulfilment of which is the very purpose of man's existence, and for which all the others are but a preparation. This is variously described by the Shivapuri Baba as God-Realization, Knowledge of Truth, Knowledge of God, the Meaning of Life and the attainment of God. Here neither Intelligence nor Mind will help us; only Faith can avail. Man can never find God, but, as in the story of the boy Dhruva, he can bring God to him if he has the required qualities of mind. Thus, though Mind and Intelligence cannot find God, they must be in the right condition if God is to be known.

In my own talks with the Shivapuri Baba, I was particularly impressed by his insistence upon the autonomy of the three disciplines. Each has a different field and different aim. With Intellect, we conquer this world and achieve earthly happiness, *sukha*. By Mind, we conquer ourselves and achieve serenity, *santosh*, and the assurance of eternal bliss. By Faith, we allow ourselves to be conquered by God, and in losing all to find all, that is Shanti. World-Realization, Soul-Realization and God-Realization are three distinct end-points of three distinct processes. A man can attach himself to any or all of these, but it is useless for him to go straight to God-Realization if he has a dull intellect and a weak mind. If he attaches himself to World-Realization he will have a happy and successful life, but death will end it all. If he attaches himself to Soul-Realization he will attain eternal bliss, but this will remain conditioned by existence. When the worlds pass away, his bliss will end and he will find that he has got nowhere. Therefore, only God-Realization is objectively and absolutely valid as the end and aim of existence.

A man may develop his intellect to the highest degree possible for a human being; this does not mean only the power of thought, but all the functions and powers associated with earthly existence. He will be able to command all kinds of existing things and beings, and assure himself of genuine happiness. But this will not, of itself, give him a strong and pure mind. He may have all the powers and yet be lost morally, and so condemned to miserable states of existence after death. He may not be morally degraded, and yet he will not have that strong vessel that can retain its content after death.

Therefore, even if his state is not miserable, it will be unsubstantial like that of a ghost. His Jiwa will be obliged to seek another vessel in order to continue its course.

The condition of a man with a strong mind, formed by discipline and the practice of virtue, is altogether more favourable. But if he lacks intelligence, he will be unable to deal with the problems of life and he will be distracted from his true aim of finding God. He may not even be able to grasp the distinction between Nirvikalpa Samādhi, that is simple bliss, and God-Realization. Thus he will easily be led astray.

Even the combination of a keen intelligence and a strong mind will not suffice to bring us to God. For that a third and completely different process must be set in motion. This process goes by the general name of meditation.

The answer already quoted to the sisters who asked him how to come to the knowledge of God, summarizes the whole teaching.

S.B. Think of God alone. Put every other thought from your mind. When all else disappears you will see God. In a flash.

Since few mortals have the strength of mind to follow this precept literally from the start, we must go by stages. There are three of these, conveniently described by the Sanskrit words dhāranā, dhyāna and samādhi, or steadiness, meditation and diffuse contemplation. In the reply given to the Hindu pupil, part of which has already been quoted, the following was said:

Q. Could you give me some hints on meditation?

S.B. Meditation has three stages, viz., Samādhi, Dhyāna and Dhāranā. Samādhi is concentration on Truth. Dhyāna is thinking of any one particular object for a long time. Dhāranā is thinking of Truth historically. In another sense, meditation is profound thinking. It makes our health better, gives extremely helpful ideas, and is quite essential for our spiritual progress. Meditation is a mad man's business. So it is best to have a separate room for it. It should be clean and neat. Artistic pictures of Rama, Krishna and other realized souls can be kept there for the sake of inspiration. Incense-burning and sacrificial fires can also be taken to, for they purify both air and mind.

Q. What is the best time for meditation?

S.B. Early in the morning. After answering the call of nature and taking a bath, simple pranayama (breath control) should be taken twice or thrice (though not more than ten times a day). An easy posture should then be occupied, with body totally erect, and meditation begun.

Q. Are meditation and concentration the same thing?

S.B. Yes, because both signify single-minded consciousness. No, because in meditation there is consciousness of both external world and internal world while in concentration there is consciousness of internal world only.

Q. What is your idea about morality?

S.B. Conceptions of morality differ according to time and place. For maintaining the Right Life, we can break any rule of morality. The universal morality is to commit no act of omission or commission. We must not be dogmatic about other forms of morality. Social stability should be maintained even against moral laws.

Q. Where can we find teachings about the Right Life at their best?

S.B. In the four Vedas. In the Ramayana, the Bhāgavat and the Mahābhārata also. But always remember that teachings found in books are only general. Particular aspirants need the guidance of a teacher, who is a realized soul.

Right Life and Meditation is a path not denying life, but making it. By accepting life and leading it in the right path, we are able to establish life and make ourselves capable of realizing the Truth by Meditation. One cannot renunciate life, if one wants to solve the problems of life, because one has to perform the threefold duties which are ordained by God. Renunciation will mean running away from life and therefore running away from its problems. The deeper meaning of life is lost by the so-called renunciation. It may, however, be mentioned here that one who has solemnly vowed to find God or Death may renounce the worldly life and go to the forest for Meditation. Meditation is also possible in leading this life. A person may meditate while performing his duties, or in a forest. But even in leading a life in a forest, one has to perform the threefold duties. A life in the forest is not a life of penance or *yogavyas*. The person seeking Truth in a forest, has to make his life by practising the 'Right Life' and having direct meditation on God.

The path of Right Living is difficult and is more easily described than followed. Each action of the external senses must be measured, and no commission or omission should be made. As we measure and make our coat, so also should we measure and make our life. The measurement should neither be longer nor shorter than is required. Only if our life is exactly regulated, will we have the time and energy required for meditation. Right meditation cannot be based upon a disordered life.

First Stage Dhāranā

This means literally the act of holding in the mind, and also of memorizing and keeping the mind collected. The word dhāranā is very ancient; it was used by the sages who compiled the Rig Veda thousands of years ago in the same sense as it is used by the

Shivapuri Baba. It is in fact the universally recognized practice of devotional exercises. Speaking to me personally as a Catholic, the Shivapuri Baba specially recommended frequent use of the rosary, the contemplation of lives of the saints, reading the Bible and verbal prayer. Tarzie Vittachi, though brought up as a Buddhist, was advised to study the Sermon on the Mount.

It is unnecessary to give further examples since *Dhāranā* is a part of all spiritual life at all times and in all religions. Its purpose is to produce an orientation of the mind that facilitates the next stages.

The Second Stage Dhyāna

This is the form of meditation by means of representation or the creation of a mental image. The corresponding word in the Sufi terminology is *tasawwur*, which means the same and has the same object. The mind is concentrated upon a specific image until the Reality behind the image becomes manifest. This is the first opening of the higher consciousness that eventually will lead us beyond consciousness itself. I cannot do better than quote a beautiful passage from one of the Shivapuri Baba's own talks.

S.B. The sole purpose of this human life is nothing but the realization of God. Meditate on Him with as much reverence and love as you can on His manifested form in the beginning. Imagine Him as standing just in front of you, His crown more dazzling than the sun's splendour, His red eyes beaming like a lotus, His neck covered all over with precious pearl necklaces, Kaustuva ornaments and vanamala, His four hands holding the conch, disc, Kaumodaki gada and the lotus, wearing the yellow pitambara, His body of amiable blue colour, His face smiling His merciful smile, His age charming like that of a young boy ready to confer blessings upon His devotees. This is called His Form as Vasudeva. Meditate on this Form repeatedly. Forget all except Him. Speak to Him, 'O God, bless me'. Speak, cry, laugh, dance, do anything, let flow your ecstatic tears. From Him is this all. Without Him there is nothing. Have a posture so as to make your mind steady on this Form. If the entire form is not possible for you to imagine within a single sweep of your vision, imagine Him in parts from head to foot. Practise like this repeatedly. Devote as much of your time as possible. Offer Him flowers, incense and bow down to His gracious feet. When your concentration on this Form fails, come down to dhāranā, let your imagination play in His sportful Līlas, in such studies as pertain to Him alone. Then again a fresh assault of concentrating on Him. Come down to dhāranā again, a fresh assault again. Go on like this for years and years. Imagine Him standing close to you as your shadow in all your thoughts and doings. Then a time will come when you will actually see Him before you. Your joy will know no bounds. Your ignorance, all this pleasure and pain will vanish. Your whole outlook will be changed.

Innumerable descriptions of the same kind are to be found in the lives of Ramakrishna and other Indian saints. Here again, it is unnecessary to give further examples.

Third Stage Samādhi

This means to be established in the identical, that is, the state of unity of subject and object: in this case the individual Purusha and the Supreme Reality.

We must beware of mistaking Dhyāna for Samādhi. In the conversation just quoted, after the Shivapuri Baba had extolled the wonder of direct awareness of the Presence of the Personal God, he went on to say:

S.B. Beware here again. Do not stop here alone. This is not all. Again there is Samādhi, the question as to whence is this Being. Stop here and seek beyond—the Unknown Source. This Being is but the assumed Form by that Unknown Source. Go and know That. There a real peep into the Vacuum happens. Then all is over. The Ultimate Goal is reached.

In another talk, he emphasized the impotence of man when he comes to the third and final stage. Until then he has to rely on his intelligence and discrimination to order his life, and upon his faith and thirst for God to sustain him in his meditation. However strong these three may be, they will not take him to the goal.

S.B. This realization can be had only by the Grace of God. Only such a man who works along this line of Swadharma, i.e. along these three principles, and yet does not get involved in enjoying the fruits thereof, and dedicates all to God, and always remains for the most part of his time in deep hankering after God, is the person who deserves this Grace.

When this self-realization comes there is nothing unaccomplished for the man. He becomes all-knowing. Even by the mere strength of his thought, things in gross states can be realized at once. There is no inertia, or seemingly long expanse of time and space, between his thought and the actual resultant matter involved. He has not even to work anything with the outside world to fulfil his thought.

In Samādhi itself there are different degrees, and the seeker after ultimate Truth must beware of the temptation to remain at some intermediate stage which, by its intense bliss and sense of liberation from all earthly ties, may appear to be the end. A man, by diligent practice of the three stages of Dhāranā, Dhyāna and Samādhi, may succeed in isolating himself completely from the external world. The advice of the Shivapuri Baba at this point is rather in the form of an account of what will happen to the man whose mind is strong enough to go right through to the end.

S.B. The man who has turned his face like this from the external creation, remains for the time being in Samādhi, which, when taken to the highest possible, becomes Nirvikalpa Samādhi. There, the man enjoys extreme bliss since there is no creation or the creational process for him. He is no longer himself involved. Here he stops. This is all, he thinks, and remains enjoying supreme happiness. This is the final goal, according to the Sānkhyas. They say that the sun, the moon, etc., and the universe are nothing but parts of one universal God. Nothing beyond this. This is all, they say. All other teachings go up to this. They take this as the Ultimate. Here man is deceived. He gets satisfied with this stage of supreme happiness. But one day it dissolves with the dissolution of the world. So there is no permanent happiness there also. Only later he comes to realize this. He finds himself kept at bay. He has left the external world and stepped into 'unknown waters'.

He knows that this coming back to life is again the same unwanted place which he has deliberately rejected and at the same time he could not gain any firm ground beyond. He is then in utmost despair. He cries for help. That shows he has now come to believe that there is some unseen Hand to help him, the Hand of God. There, in that utter helplessness, he gets stirred. If not, while in Nirvikalpa Samādhi, he remains completely at rest and enjoys supreme bliss. This stirring, but no coming back, must necessarily drive him beyond where he is, in that utter despair. Consequently one-pointed attention is taken to the climax and the Flash happens. He gets the Vision. He sees himself. Only then the real life of the man begins.

The realistic and practical turn he gave to every question—even when speaking of Final Realization—is shown in a message he sent me through Thakur Lal in reply to a letter about difficulties in steadying the mind.

S.B. This, of course, is in everybody's case in the beginning stages. Do not get disheartened. Remain in Dhāranā, Dhyāna and Samādhi. What is Dhāranā? Think of Christ, for instance, remember His teachings His personality, His life-activities and all that you know of Him. Also think of the Sun, the Moon or the stars or rivers, mountains, lakes, etc., which are the creation of God. Read Scriptures and the like. Say prayers. Tell the beads. Thus go on thinking of the glories of God in one way or another, so that you spend your time on God and nothing else. This is Dhāranā, where you remain, as if in a bigger circle. This too is a form of meditation. Go on and think what is the meaning of life. By thus doing you try to penetrate into the mysteries of God. This is Dhyāna, where you get more concentrated. Then again when you make such inquiries as 'Who am I?' you come to concentrate as if on a point (from the bigger circle of Dhyāna and Dhāranā). This process of Dhārānā, Dhyāna and Samādhi is to be repeated times without number. By thus doing your mind is forcibly made to stay on God and in course of time, say, in months or years your mind must get tamed and become steady. In Samādhi, of course, one's mind cannot at present stand even for a fraction of a second; only in course of time you will succeed. Distaste for life and continued practice of

115

meditation on God is the only qualification needed. Mind's desire is to be curbed. External duties should be planned definitely and critically observed. Avoid every work outside this. Successfully do what is planned. Without God-Realization nothing is possible. The only object should be *that*!

CHAPTER FIVE

NEW LIGHTS ON OLD TEACHINGS

IN this chapter, I propose to bring together a number of utterances by the Shivapuri Baba relating specifically to Indian philosophy and practice. These are taken almost entirely from the notes provided by Thakur Lal Manandhar.

The discussions turn upon the two main schools which taught, and still teach, the way of life according to the Vedas and Brahmanas. These are Sānkhya, founded by Kapila probably in the sixth century B.C., and Yoga, commonly associated with the name of Patanjali, who lived several centuries later. There are also many references to the three chief philosophical systems. The first is Dvaita, or dualism, which maintains that God and the world, Brahman and the material Universe, the Supreme Being and the Individual Soul are both real and different from one another. The second system, associated with the name of the great sage and saint, Shankara, who lived in the eighth century of our era, is Advaita, or non-dualism. This asserts the formula already quoted of Shankara, "Brahman alone is real. The world is unreal. The Individual soul (Atman) is identical with the Supreme (Brahman)." The third system is that of Ramanuja, who lived in the tenth century. It is known as *Viśiṣthadvaita*, or advanced non-dualism, inasmuch as it asserts that Brahman the Absolute Being and Prakriti the Universe are both real but identical. It can be called absolute pantheism.

The Shivapuri Baba takes his stand upon the Bhagavad Gita, and even claims that his teaching is that of the Gita brought up to date to suit the conditions of modern life. In his comments he often implies an argument based on the authority of the Gita. The following example is taken from one of the earlier conversations with Manandhar:

S.B.:

Advaita. If the object in view comes all right to the required level or standard, the religion or life must come in automatically. So the object only, that is, peace of mind, is to be maintained. Thus much importance is given to the object only by this school of thought.

Dvaita. Religion or life is the most important thing because without this, the object in view, that is peace of mind, cannot be accomplished.

Visiśthadvaita. Both are equally important. With either of them only, the other may not necessarily come all right.

But for a wise man the theories of all the three schools are incorrect. If the object only is kept in view our propaganda is overlooked, and the object cannot be maintained up to the required standard. Also, even if religion or propaganda only is maintained, the object may not come all right. Again, if both are maintained, even then, the maintenance up to our satisfaction may be a failure. The five causes come between, namely: Fate (God), time, place, circumstances and the presiding Divinity.

This is a reference to the eighteenth and last chapter of the Gita, which applies the lessons of all the systems to the practical problem confronting Arjuna. The Shivapuri Baba illustrates the theme by the simple example of the buying of flowers for him, described in Chapter Two.

To maintain our peace of mind or a balanced state of our being we need to accept a certain code of living, which we call religion. Giving this example of keeping flowers, he said: "Maintaining the flowers is the object in view, and the arrangement we make, that is, our propaganda in spending a fixed amount of money, a fixed labour or effort spent in a fixed time, is the religion. The work as a whole is life, which may be a successful one or a failure."

S.B. One must pray to God, since fate or God may not be favourable. As to time, if the flower is out of season we may not get the required quantity of flowers and may fail to maintain our object which is to keep the flowers. In India, at this time of the year you would not be able to get this particular kind. And in adverse circumstances also, we may fail to maintain this keeping of flowers.

While preserving the characteristic Indian doctrine that the goal of all existence is to return to the Absolute Source, he is completely practical in his treatment of the situation as it confronts us all, saint and sinner alike. Whether the world is real or not, we have to deal with it. The following talk is delightful in its combination of matter of fact realism and acceptance of the transcendental character of the aim.

S.B. There is a vast difference in knowing a thing and in having it. Knowledge of a thing is not necessarily the realization of it. For instance, we know that there is such a country as England which is so and so. But this knowledge itself is not the realization of it. Likewise, for a real aspirant after truth, the simple knowledge gained of it alone can do no good. Such a knowledge we can have from the writings of the great thinkers of the world, the Vedas and the Upanishads. Suppose we have gone through all of them and gained knowledge of the truth, does this mean that we have realized it? Yes, we have done what we can to gain the knowledge. But with simply this we do not get satisfied. We can still assume that there is something beyond and there is a longing for that. How to attain that? Leaders of thought there are many, each preaching his own system of procedure. Whom to believe? We become puzzled as to the immediate step. Advaitins say: 'Leave off this love for life and seek beyond,' thus emphasizing the necessity of complete renunciation of the external world. If not, what is all this? Our life at every moment demands something or other from the outside. This hunger, thirst and the rest will always be pricking us from the external world. There is something unpleasant in this mode of life. After all, this theory is not at all intelligent as far as its practicability is concerned.

S.B. Again, Dvaitins advise us quite the opposite. This is all, they say, this life and its enjoyments in the material world. Live and enjoy is their motto. All right, let us assume, we take to living and enjoying this life. But does this make us satisfied? The objects we enjoy are not always with us. They come and go. We enjoy sometimes, and suffer at another time painfully. No stability of mind is assured in this either. How can we go on taking this mode of life? This kind of life is not at all reasonable, we discover.

S.B. In short, Advaita advocates Jñana or non-attachment (spiritual discipline), Visishadvaita advocates Bhakti or right behaving (moral discipline), and Dvaita, Karma or physical discipline. Thus there are many schools of thought or reasonableness. Each of them has remodelled truth according to its own pattern.

S.B. The only reasonable exposition of truth or knowledge as it is, is that which we can find in the Vedas, since they try to give us knowledge or understanding of what we see and hear in this world, as lucidly as possible. What is to be admired most, is that they neither forcibly thrust upon us any creed or doctrine, nor do they ever advise us not to accept a creed. They simply expose knowledge, and allow us to go on as we like. Here, in this Vedic teaching, we find sufficient reasonableness, in as much as we can take any course to suit our personal case. But as beginners or immature people, we can get only knowledge as exposed in them, and yet remain in a puzzle. Only our spiritual guide, or Guru, can reveal to us the real import of those teachings.

S.B. Therefore, a life according to Yajna, Dāna and Tapas, which together make Swadharma or 'Right Life', is the best and the most reasonable also. Our external life will be well managed, and consequently there will be no disturbings from life. We are then left free to think of the beyond, our supreme goal.

S.B. A piece of iron is drawn towards the magnet. This world with all objects is external, tempting us as by a magnet, and if we allow it we are doomed. But if some orange juice or something is poured over the magnet its action is neutralized. So also Yajna, Dāna and Tapas is such a thing as will neutralize the effect of this world temptation.

He spoke on the necessary prerequisites required to practise this kind of life. The first requisite is independence of action. The second is independence from one's own ignorance. The third is independence to strive after God-Realization. The independence of action is to be brought about by mere brute force, and the other two by the practice of virtues and charity.

He gave the following criticism of the Sānkhya theory of Māyā and of the nature of the liberation of Purusha.

S.B. Purusha plays with Māyā, which is a combination of His strength and intelligence. This creates consciousness, which is adrishta—unseen or vague—avyakta. This in turn produces *Vyakta*, i.e. a distinct idea of itself with name and form. Then comes Knowledge, intellect and the rest. If the Purusha does not play with Māyā, no *avyakta* or consciousness is formed, and consequently no involvement for Him with the process of the twenty-four principles. The result is a complete standstill, and so there is supreme happiness for the Purusha.

S.B. This state of being for the Purusha is quite unnatural, though there is no doubt as to its possibility, because he is in one line with the world whose nature too is all happiness. He is, so to say, dissolved in this world-being. So when the world will have its end, as it must one day, he too will have to disappear. Consequently, it is proved that he cannot attain his identification with the Self or God. That is why this theory has been refuted by Gita and Brahma sutra.

Refutation

S.B. This samādhi, or the supreme happiness of the aforementioned theory, will end one day. The man then is nowhere. Realization of Self or God is not attained. So we need not reject the playing with Māyā as it is called, i.e. the use of the strength and intelligence we have in us, in as much as it serves in the maintenance or preservation of this body, which comes under Swadharma. The continuous thought of God, who is behind us, is maintained; and, in using our strength and intelligence, a mere defensive attitude is kept, and then only we can rest assured that we are not involved in the working of the twenty-four principles.

S.B. To sum up: The Sānkhya theory of Māyā—only full happiness in samādhi—one's dissolution together with the dissolution of the world. Gita's refutation of it—playing with Māyā is allowed in Swadharma—but beware! Only turn to God not to happiness—Anāśakti yoga according to Gita.

The Bhagavad Gita, in Chapter XIII, contains a summary of the elaborate cosmology derived from the Vedas and developed in the Upanishads and the Brahmasūtras. The purpose is to distinguish between the objective element of experience (Kshetra) and the subjective element (Purusha). The *Kshetra* is in its primitive significance the human body with its functions and powers; but it is also prakriti, the body of the universe. The thirteenth chapter of the Gita abounds in beautiful expressions of the nature of the object, the subject and of knowledge itself, but it does not bring them into any obvious connection with the aim of God-Realization. The Shivapuri Baba recasts the material in the form of answers to the three eternal questions Why? How? and What?

Why?—To attain bliss: *Ānanda*.

This has three forms. One is pleasure *Sukha* which belongs to the body, Kshetra. The second is *Santosh* which is serenity of mind, Manas. The third is *Shanti* or peace of the inner self, that is, Purusha.

The why of all activity consists in the attainment of one of the three forms of bliss.

How?—By purified awareness: *Citta*.

This also has three forms:

Physical Discipline which brings pleasure

Moral Discipline which brings serenity

Spiritual Discipline which brings peace

What?—That which is: *Sat*.

This has three categories:

(1) Transcendental: God, Purusha and Māyā.

(2) The Modes: Unmanifest (Avyakta)
    Manifest (vyakta) Mind (manas)

(3) Intellect and the rest of the twenty-four principles, namely
    Intellect
    1—feeling
    5 inner senses
    5 outer senses
    5 objects of sense

and the five great elements.

The first three are called the Suddha tattwas, which lead to the knowledge of God that is *Samādhi*.

The second set of three are the Madhyama tattwas, which

bring power, that is *Siddhi*. The remainder are the Adhama tattwas, which bring *Gaddi*, or Kingship.

The point is that the three groups relate to the three disciplines and indicate the objects to which the attention is directed in each case. As we reflect upon the question what? we find that we are just as powerless to grasp it in the domain of Intellect as we are in those of Mind and Will.

The Shivapuri Baba nevertheless shows how the entire scheme can serve to guide us in the right direction if only we are resolute in our inquiry. He explains it as follows:

S.B. All the things we see in this universe, men, and materials, all nature and its different phenomena, are simply bewildering. We cannot make out what they are. The reality behind them, the secret of secrets is quite hidden to our view and, as it were, hermetically sealed. The earnest inquirer is times without number repelled from his activity, thrown back into despair and anxiety as he cannot come to a right solution of all this bewildering complexity.

S.B. If we do not lose heart and patiently continue our searching, our earnest inquiry will naturally have a right direction, we find a real Guru who is self-realized. When rightly approached he gives a satisfactory answer to our query. His analysis of this existence and ourself comes under the head of twenty-four principles or tattwas, viz. God, Purusha and Māyā; then come the unseen fate (avyakta), the same with name (vyakta), mind or knowledge which gives form to the unseen force and makes it distinct; last come Intellect, and the five tanmatras, and finally the five external and five internal Indriyas. The first three are the Suddha tattwas or pure principles, the next three, the Madhyama tattwas and the rest are the Adhama tattwas.

S.B. God is like an infinite mass of water, while Purusha is a finite quantity of the same water; as a small piece of sugar is but a part of an infinite mass of sugar, while the quality in both the cases remains the same. This Purusha within us called Jivatman is a descent from God or Paramatman, a part of Him but full in itself like Him. And this Purusha, unlike inert matter, plays with his strength and intelligence, which both together are called Māyā.

123

This playing, or the application of his strength and intelligence, is the cause for the effects to be formed. The effects are the Madhyama and Adhama tattwas. How? This playing with Māyā effects a sort of Fate which in the beginning is unseen, then becomes seen and named, and again this mind or knowledge makes it perfectly clear or distinct. In short a name and form is given to that Avyakta. Then this Intellect resolves to materialize this kind of knowledge. It plans and gives the order to the five tanmatras and Indryas to execute. This is how this existence came to be formed, and what we see around us is this playing of the Purusha with Māyā and the different effects cast on the canvas.

S.B. Naturally, then we come to ask why is this all? There must be a purpose behind all this working. The answer we get is that all this is for the enjoyment of the Purusha—for his own happiness, so to say. This perfect happiness is composed of Sukha, Santosh and Shanti, that is, pleasure, serenity and peace. If any one of these is lacking, we cannot call our happiness perfect. How can we get this and always enjoy Supreme Bliss which is our real nature? That is the question we must keep before us.

In another conversation, he spoke again about the tattwas, or elements, which enter into our total experience. We cannot be aware directly of the transcendental elements until the moment of Supreme Vision is vouchsafed to us. Then we see God as God, ourselves as Purusha, and the whole universe as Prakriti. The triple vision is a single vision because we see the One Reality in its three aspects that is represented by these three words.

Meanwhile, our point of departure must be the experience that is given to us in our present state.

The Adhama tattwas include the senses, inner and outer, and their objects. They constitute the apparatus with which the mind is provided so that it can do its work. They must be distinguished from the contents of the mind, which are the twenty-six virtues and the corresponding vices.

The sensitive apparatus is the ten Indriyas. The objects are the Bhūtas. Their role in the working of the mind is described in the following talk:

S.B. Mind is the officer-in-charge of the ten Indriyas, while

Intellect is in charge of the ten Bhūtas. Indriyas come in contact with the Bhūtas and if mind does not restrict their conduct, they play as they like. If Mind is not strong enough to guard itself against the influences of rāga and dwesha, the Indriyas will go on playing with the Bhūtas as they like or dislike. This should not be allowed. Mind should restrict the conduct of the Indriyas. This behaving of the Indriyas with the Bhūtas is done by Intellect. Mind will prescribe the conduct, and the prescribed conduct is performed by the Intellect. What to speak and what not to speak, what to do and what not to do, what to think and what not to think—these must be decided. If this much is observed, our mind and our intellect both work in perfect order. For example, such and such a sound is to be heard by the ear, and such and such an amount of space only is to be used. Like this, both the gross and the subtle Bhūtas are to be prescribed for use by the Indriyas. This is what we call restriction put in the workings of the intellect. If mind allows rāga or dwesha to interfere, this prescribed working of the intellect will not be possible. The Bhūtas are of three kinds. Of them sattwic ones only are to be used as material. The three kinds must be well known and recognized. In this working, Egoism must keep aloof and not interfere.

The distinction between Intellect and Mind comes in again. Intellect is for the outer world, mind is for inner strength and purity. Knowledge of the world is *tattwa jñana*.

S.B. Intellect rules over the ten Bhūtas, and Mind over the ten Indriyas. The ten Indriyas coming in contact with the ten Bhūtas is what we call Karma or activity. In Right Life, this Karma is restricted by allowing neither Akarma nor Vikarma to enter. This is done by restricting ourselves to such actions only—that is so much karma—as will do no harm to this body and its belongings. Indriyas playing with the Bhūtas is restricted. What to speak, what not to speak, what to do and what not, what to think and what not, the sense behind such a way of living.

S.B. We should know all the ingredients of the Bhūtas, as we know all the ingredients of our meals to be cooked. We speak, touch, think or understand, take interest and resolve in the case of the subtle Bhūtas. In like manner, we behave with the gross Bhūtas also. Intellect restricts the Bhūtas and Mind controls the Indriyas. In a sense, mind should not allow raga or dwesha to come and influence the Intellect.

S.B. The truth is that what we work with is this mind and intellect and the five Indriyas. And as everything outside is composed of the five elements, we have in our body the same elements in the form of these Indriyas. Our thought can thus create things from within ourselves. That is why it is the decision of scientists that this world is a continuous thought. We think of the required sort of things: we give voice to it. Naturally sound is produced. This sound in turn cannot remain without producing air or motion. This air in turn produces a definite direction in the domain of water, and this in turn creates fire, or zeal in fulfilment, and lastly comes earth, or a definite or concrete form fulfilled.

S.B. The following sequence illustrates the creative process at work in the mind.

1. The thought arises "I shall to to Dhruvasthali". The idea is vaguely heard. This is sound or ether.
2. The implication becomes clear and takes form. "I am in contact with it." This is touch or air.
3. "I am moved to action. A decision arises in me." This is form or fire.
4. The action now holds my attention and interest. "I am engaged in it." Taste or water.
5. "I now am realizing the object. I am on the way." Smell or earth. "I reach Dhruvasthali." Subject and Object become One. The creative act is accomplished.

S.B. The Indriyas and the Bhūtas have their proximate and ultimate sources in the three gunas or qualities of Nature. Sattwa. Sources of life for the Indriyas such as sun, moon, etc. Rajas— Citta, manas, buddhi, ahamkāra and the ten Indriyas. Tamas— The five elements and the five objects of sense—sound, ether or sky (hearing) touch, air (knowing) form fire or light (seeing) taste water (liking) smell earth (realizing).

When asked more about the tattwas or elements he said:

S.B. There are different opinions as regards the number of the tattwas. But for our purpose, God or 'this existence' is the only tattwa. This existence, which we see externally and internally as well, is nothing but God. This 'I' should go on inquiring 'What is this?' This is meditation or God-Concentration. This is Atma-tattwas, or soul, of which we have our own awareness. This awareness is under the influence of the three gunas. Next there is our experience of existence. This experience is gained through Intellect. Now, what is imperative is that this intellect and the resultant experience is to be made limited, that is, to run on a particular channel. Unless we limit we cannot apprehend because this experience itself is infinite. For a man after God it must be limited. When Akarma and Vikarma are eradicated and only Karma remains, there is right experience or Sukha. Since the working of the intellect is controlled, this Sukha is also well-controlled, and as a result we are saved from being lost in the infinite expanse of Sukha.

On another occasion, he spoke about the five subtle elements. *S.B.* God we do not see. We see only this existence. What do we mean by 'this existence'. It is the platform upon which we stand and try to get a peep towards God, who is beyond. This is problem number one. It has come out of this existence—which is zero. Problem number two is Right Living—Swadharma—which is to help us towards the solution of problem number one. The third problem is to find the right channels through which to run this Swadharma, failing which we come into conflict with the externals.

Thus we have now come up to five principles:

(1) God	∞	Infinity
(2) Existence	0	Zero
(3) The problem of existence	1	Monad
(4) Swadharma	2	Dyad
(5) The right channels which are the three disciplines, physical, moral and spiritual	3	Triad

These are the five tattwas or elements in their subtle sense.

S.B. Again, there is element number six which comprises: study, practice of the virtues and charity, holy association (sat-sang), service to the teacher (guru-seva). All these come under this number six. By these various means we make some contribution— in a stray manner so to say—in order to get qualified for admission to the group of five. Although this sixth element is outside the group, it ought to be given a place.

S.B. You remember the story of the *Asvins*. In the Vedas, they are the bringers of health. Why do we want the Asvins? We want health, not the Asvins. But the Asvins stand for healing. If we have not yet got health, then we must have healing in order to qualify for admission among healthy people. In the same way, if we have not Swadhaıma yet, we must do number six in order to qualify for Right Living.

S.B. What we have to attain is God. This is possible only through this existence before us. We need, therefore, only God (infinity) and this existence (zero) for our purpose. What makes us take recourse to monad, dyad and triad?

S.B. If you are given the order 'take meals': taking meals is the only work that has to be done. What makes us take to collecting materials and go about cooking? We cannot eat until the food is prepared. Obviously therefore these three—monad, dyad and triad, namely, the problem of existence, swadharma and the three disciplines, serve as auxiliaries to God and zero.

S.B. To attempt to stand on those two alone would be something like standing upon the point of a needle. Not everyone is strong enough for that and so we need an aid. On the basis of this very argument, by taking to physical, moral and spiritual disciplines, we keep our Swadharma intact. By doing Swadharma, we again face the problem of existence.

S.B. Consequently, our being face to face with the problem of Right Living means that we take good care of this zero—that is Existence—and this Infinity—that is God.

In this remarkable utterance, the saint bridges the gap between Indian spirituality, exclusively concerned with God, and Western practicality, exclusively concerned with the needs of this world. Swadharma, or Right Living, is more than a *pis aller*, a compromise with human weakness: it becomes one of the five subtle elements from which Reality is to be forged. The sixth element, which comprises all kinds of good practices and spiritual exercises, is outside the basic pentad, but should be given, as it were, a complimentary ticket for the banquet in the capacity of the cook who has prepared the food. The assertion that Right Living is the bond between zero, that is Existence, and infinity, that is God, is a formula that would be acceptable to any believer of whatever creed and to all who follow the perennial philosophy in the search for Truth.

I have myself introduced the terms: monad, dyad and triad corresponding to the problem of life, right living and the three disciplines. Students of Systematics will note the remarkable aptness of the Shivapuri Baba's descriptions. Those who are not familiar with Systematics and wish to inquire further can find a brief account in the Introduction to Volume Two of my *Dramatic Universe*. The Shivapuri Baba used simply the numbers one, two and three which evidently refer to one-, two- and three-term systems.

Sānkhya and Yoga

The following extracts from talks preserved by Manandhar deal with the two schools of practical spirituality most in vogue. These are the ways of withdrawal and struggle: the ever-present dilemma of Hamlet, 'whether 'tis better in the mind to suffer the slings and arrows of outrageous fortune, or to take arms against a sea of troubles and, by opposing, end them.' Here the 'sea of troubles' is Saṁsāra, and the 'slings and arrows' are the Adhama tattwas, or coarse elements of our sense experience, and the ceaseless activity within the mind.

The following talk is given exactly as recorded by Manandhar:
S.B. Modern Science, with all its achievements, is now baffled with bigger problems in Nature. For instance, it now speaks of Cosmic Rays which it tries to explain, but fails, in as much as it speaks only of *How* they are and cannot describe *what* they are in reality. Science has, so to say, in its striving after Reality, had a

turning here from the differentiated consciousness to Undifferentiated consciousness. All other rays, such as the sun's rays and those of other stars and planets, are differentiated in terms of consciousness, while Cosmic rays are undifferentiated. Science, therefore, has achieved transcendence from Māyā to Mahāmāyā. Scientists, while explaining what the Cosmic rays are, say that they are extraterritorial and so they are baffling to the scientific mind. They fail to explain what they are.

S.B. In ancient India, we had two main systems of philosophy— one, the Sānkhya theory of Kapila, and the other the Yoga system of Patanjali. The former in its exposition of its theory enjoins upon us to ignore Māyā, or the differentiated consciousness, and to remain in Mahāmāyā, or the Undifferentiated consciousness. One who follows this Sānkhya theory in practice therefore comes to a stage where he is immune from the differentiated consciousness and where complete peace and harmony prevail.

S.B. Yoga, on the other hand, propounds its theory in a different way. It asks us to resist this differentiated consciousness in Nature by gaining power, or *siddhi*, with the help of the different yogic *sādhanas*, and so to command peace and happiness. So, in trying to remedy the evils and sufferings in the world for humanity, these two systems both lead us to a state of peace and happiness in the undifferentiated consciousness. The Gita and Brahmasūtra therefore come forward and denounce both these systems of philosophy, for the simple reason that they could only lead humanity up to a certain point. Peace and harmony, which is achieved by the Sānkhya way, tumble down at times when death and dissolution come upon humanity, and the pleasure and happiness achieved by the Yoga theory, too, meet with the same fate.

S.B. What Gita and Brahmasūtra aim at is God-knowledge, by attaining which we have freedom from ignorance. God, who is beyond both the differentiated and the undifferentiated consciousness of being, alone can give a final solution of all the problems we are confronted with. According to this theory, we can establish our direct communion with God from start to finish. This is the only right life where the problem of problems is solved.

S.B. While establishing this communion with God we need, in the early stages, to have an amicable settlement with the differentiated as well as the undifferentiated consciousness of being. Unlike the Sānkhyas, the doctrine of Swadharma—Right Living—advocates only the idea of taming our mind, since in ignoring this there is a perpetual strain on the aspirant who may at times succumb to it. In the other system, that is Yoga, the same lack of wisdom and foresight is again found, because, even if we let man acquire the highest power by yogic *sadhanas*, he is like a Lilliputian in the presence of a higher power.

S.B. Resistance to Nature is the idea of the *yogin*, but, in the long run, it falls flat before an overwhelmingly superior force. Thus, in trying to attain God or final deliverance, these two systems have only devised ways and means to counteract the forces of our being in Nature. They do so in their own way, and so lose themselves on the way without attaining the final Goal, just like a river coming out from a desert and disappearing in the same desert.

S.B. The theory of Right Life, as expounded by Gita, is like a river running to a big ocean of God-knowledge. But as these two systems, though found defective, can serve as aids for a man of Right Life in taming his mind and intelligence, and as they form part of his training sometimes by ignoring and sometimes by resisting, they have been given a place in the curriculum of Swadharma or Right Life.

The Shivapuri's criticism of Yoga, that it seeks to turn back the stream of Saṁsāra or to overcome Nature, impressed me very favourably. When I first studied the Yoga Shāstra of Patanjali and read the famous third verse: *Yogaschitta vritti nirodha:* Yoga is constraint placed on the fluctuations of the mind-stuff, I was, at first, convinced that this was the right way. It seemed to agree with Gurdjieff's formula: Struggle without mercy with your negative principles and you will be saved.

Later I came to realize that there is a great difference between trying to do the whole work oneself and confining the 'struggle' to the rejection of the impulses coming from our own 'negative principle'. When I first met the Shivapuri Baba, and he said that the only way to acquire a strong mind is to set oneself the discipline of following the impulses of our higher nature and rejecting those coming from the lower nature, I saw that he was saying exactly the same as Gurdjieff taught; and, indeed, what any spiritual director would recommend to a Christian in search of the inner life. The conviction of the identity of his teaching with what is advised in Christian spirituality was confirmed by his warning that moral discipline alone will not lead us to God—for this final step, only faith, submission to His Will, patience and waiting for the Grace of God will avail.

When I asked the Shivapuri Baba if his teaching could be regarded as a Yoga or combination of yoga ways (yoga-marga), he said that it is as beyond Yoga. The following extract from Manandhar will help to make clear what he meant:

S.B. All religions and teachings are unanimously pointing out to one Supreme Truth, or God. This life in which we are is full of shortcomings and full of imperfections. But if we go beyond we can have a perfect life. In the matter of this attainment, all religions like Christianity, Buddhism etc., and all sects and creeds like Pashupat, Vaishnavism etc., all agree. And to attain that perfection, or God, they enjoin upon us *to do* something, or *to behave* somehow, or *to know* something. Thus, in this lower aspect, which is an auxiliary to the higher attainment, they speak differently, and all these different opinions are summed up and classified in the scriptures into three main heads, namely Karma, Bhakti and Jñana.

S.B. Unfortunately, the original Brahmasūtras are now lost to us. The present day Brahmasūtra refutes each of these different sayings. It makes a survey of all the different teachings or points which they advocate, and in course of analysis it has classified all of them under these three main categories viz., Karma, Bhakti, and Jñana, and refutes each of them in these terms:

(1) By doing something (i.e., by Karma) what one achieves is only bodily welfare. While it professes to lead to the higher attainment, this process of Karma can only bring external happiness or pleasure (Sukha).

(2) By behaving in a particular way (i.e. by Bhakti) what one gains is only mental equilibrium (or Santosh).

(3) Again by knowing something (i.e. by Jñana Marga) what

we gain is only non-attachment and as a result simply peace or Shanti. God-Realization is still far away.

S.B. Thus, each proved to be insufficient and tending to something else other than God, and so is refuted one by one. What then is to be taken recourse to, which leads to God? Here Gita comes forward and takes all these three as honourable gentlemen. Each is taken full use of and advice is given to go through all of them. All three together produce a factor which tends to the one aim to which all had agreed before. When God is aimed at during these three processes, the different results particular to each of them drop off, and lose importance. They are all utilized, and in combination made to bear fruit in the shape of God attainment. Sarva Karma Phala Tyaga (every action gives fruit to be abandoned) i.e., we must never allow ourselves to be entangled in the enjoyment of the different results, before we reach our goal or realization.

Nirvikalpa Samādhi

The key notion here is that every new vantage ground reached becomes a prison if we seek to enjoy it beyond the moment it is reached. That which at one moment seems an unattainable goal, where all our hopes will be fulfilled, is at last reached, It is as full of joy as we hoped. Or else it gives us the knowledge or the power we had been longing for. In doing so it tempts us to remain. To go forward, we must abandon the joy or the knowledge or even the power that has been won. We may even say that we have come to life at last and we are asked to die to this life so hardly won. But without death there can be no resurrection. Thousands of aspirants to the highest Truth have lost their way through mistaking a milestone for the terminus.

The dangers grow greater, not less, as we go forward on the path. At the early stages our achievements, however exciting and permanent they may seem at first blush, soon begin to tarnish. They will not stand up to the test of the influences of the outer world and our own nature, and we can scarcely deceive ourselves. Later we begin to feel strong and we may mistake strength for freedom. Further on again comes the opening of higher realms of experience beyond the reach of ordinary consciousness. When we enter this realm we no longer have the objective test of external influences, because we are really free from them and do not deceive ourselves on this score. The danger is that we imagine that we have 'arrived'. The supreme bliss we experience seems to be full God-Realization and we have no wish, and imagine we have no need, to go any further. I can speak of this with assurance for I have known this temptation myself: but I never saw so clearly how it is to be recognized and overcome until I heard the Shivapuri Baba speak of it. Unfortunately, I have no record of my own talk with him on the subject, but the following extract from Manandhar is applicable to us all.

S.B. Karma, Akarma and *Vikarma* are the three classes of our activities. Akarma or useless activities and Vikarma or harmful ones must be abandoned. Only Karma or useful ones are to be well attended to. If this is found too difficult, this work of eliminating these two activities may be accomplished only gradually, according as our strength of tyaga (or spirit of renunciation) permits. In doing Karma alone, which involves a daily repetition of almost the same items of work, we naturally acquire a dexterous hand in the long run. Our relation with the outside world, that is our physical or intellectual order, will be very well established. We shall then have no complaints against the external world, since by then we shall have achieved a smooth sailing as far as our life-demands are concerned. We shall then be freely allowed to think on, or ponder over, the Absolute Truth which is beyond.

S.B. 'Who am I?' is our question. 'O God, reveal to me the secret.' Thus praying we go on with an agitated mind and spend all the rest of our time. We bow down to Him and ask for His grace and, as long as His grace does not descend upon us, we never leave this—our agitation. Quite a tedious business it is. But still we must go on, since there is no other way to be taken recourse to. To play hide and seek with the monotony there we must go on playing with either Dhāranā or Dhyāna.

S.B. But beware, when we get to improve our capability to remain in this Absolute thought for longer periods, after long practice we may begin to experience a kind of serene happiness or Bliss. That is what we call Nirvikalpa Samādhi and there, we may get entangled. We may think that as our goal, which is erroneous. That sort of thing happens only if we give way to lethargy. On the contrary, we must go on with our original question as to 'Who am I?'. As long as this Truth of truths is not revealed to us we must not stop our agitation or else we are doomed. Because there is an end to this world of blissful experience one day. This is what we term as spiritual order. There, as a river flows incessantly with a definite course to its destination, we go on flowing, as it were, with this agitation for seeing God.

S.B. In between these two orders there is a working principle which is, so to say, our mind. This mind is now in association with the three gunas, namely Sattwic, Rajasic and Tamasic. Its present association with them (as to be judged by the standard of this— our moral order) is quite illegal. Generally, for a gross understanding, Ichchhā (or desire), Rāga (or liking) and Dwesha (or hatred) can best be identified with sattwic, rajasic and tamasic states of mind respectively. A mind beyond these three states, too, can have a kind of desire. But since it is not then tainted with any other motive, except our agitation to have the Truth of truths revealed as expressed in our higher activity, and since it does not entertain any idea of indulgence in our lower activity (that is, in our relation with the external world) more than what is strictly necessary for maintaining our external life, this kind of desire is free from impurities which deteriorate our mind. When there is Rāga, or liking, and Dwesha, or hatred, in the lower sphere of our activity, we may either indulge more than what is required or less than what is necessary. In more indulgence we shall have to lose our stock of energy for nothing, and in less, too, we shall be pricked from the life-demands. In any case, we shall have to face only troubles both from above and below, and we shall be unable to maintain our balance both ways. This is why this third principle, that is, this moral order, is also a very important factor which we must never overlook.

S.B. These three principles or orders, as aforesaid, should go on side by side. Any other teachings, however brilliant they may seem to be, should not be allowed to drag us down from this— our established code of living. Far from it, they should be made, on the contrary, to serve us in promoting our own established course.

S.B. The moral principles described serves us as a yard-stick and, like an inspector, it reviews our other two activities in the most excellent manner.

The Role of the Intellect

Another way of looking at the whole process is that it consists in the liberation of the man, the True Self, the Purusha within, from the dominion of the instruments given him for his life and his search for God. We depend upon our instruments, but we need not and must not be slaves to them. Also we must know what each of them is for and not expect from an instrument what it cannot give. There is, for example, a very important distinction the Shivapuri Baba made, in his talks with us, between *Buddhi* the Natural Understanding and the *Bodha* the Spiritual Understanding. Bodha is *Intellectus*, in the sense that St. Thomas Aquinas uses the term, the one means by which the natural man can approach supernatural knowledge.

I have found a passage bearing on this theme in the notes and give it with a few corrections of language. There is a reference to the Gāyatri, the invocation that every Brahmana must repeat night and morning from the day he puts on the sacred card until he dies. The verse, taken from the Rig Veda (3.62.10), runs: 'Let us meditate upon the glorious radiance of Sāvritri. May it enlighten our Intellect.'

S.B. Whatever we do in this world is through our Intellect. It is an instrument. We are solely guided by it. If we follow its lead blindly, and, if it is wrong, it will lead us to troubles. That is why the necessity arose to perform Gāyatri daily, meaning thereby, to pray to this Intellect not to lead us astray. It is a separate unity like mind and the different Indriyas within us. It is therefore to be worshipped like a god. As a barber daily sharpens his razor blade, so as to make it well-working and thus to avoid troubles; so a sort of sharpening or making fit this intellect is a daily necessity for one who wants to avoid every trouble.

S.B. This Intellect which we now speak of is termed as Buddhi which is not perfect. We do always come to trouble if we follow its lead. There is only one Supreme Wisdom which we call Bodha. That is right and that gives us freedom from troubles. This Bodha should be made our guide. Its acquisition depends upon how far we have made our intellect pure in the light of the three disciplines. *S.B.* Our intellect should be in line with morality. Knowledge or the avoiding of the influence of the three gunas, and lastly with a careful avoidance of akarma and vikarma. For instance, you bought the watch from that person. Later now it came to be known that it is a stolen thing. The man who lost it claims to be the owner of the watch. Such a trouble came. Now let us penetrate into the matter. We did a work of buying this watch. Who brought us all this trouble? Obviously, it is this intellect through which we worked. Let us see how far this is wrong in the light of the three principles. The activity side is right since it was taken up as karma (it is neither a useless or a harmful one). Knowledge also came right because we got how good a watch we wanted. But in the last, i.e., the side or morality, we find the defect. The right morality in buying a watch we could not look into. From a recognized shop or a dealer, who is a reliable agent, we should have bought it. This idea did never strike our mind before. When one of the three principles is wrong the fact that the other two are right can have no excuse. The trouble is there already. That means that the other two are also affected and made to look wrong.

In Chapter One, I have quoted from Hugh Ripman's travel diary. The following extracts are a continuation. He started from the Gita and therefore, the Shivapuri Baba's replies, though of very general interest, are specially relevant here.

"I asked him how a man can learn to live as the first chapters of the Gita teach that one should live. He spoke about dividing the day into two: one part for carrying out necessary duties; one part for worship of God. Speaking about necessary duties, he explained that one should try not to do unnecessary things, and to do what was necessary for this reason, and not for the sake of gratifying desires. Eating, for instance: one should eat enough to give the body the energy it requires, and not more, and not because one is tempted by the taste of the food. Whatever one does, eating, walking, sitting, talking, writing, reading, thinking—everything should be done in this way, and done consciously (he emphasized this). He said with a smile that it was 'a little difficult' at first, and that it needed much practice, but that with practice it became easier.

I asked him to speak about the three gunas, or forces.

S.B. Now we are at the mercy of the three gunas. They act through us and we are their passive playthings. We have to make them our servants.

By way of example he spoke exactly like Gurdjieff—'inwardly not to identify, and outwardly, to play one's role consciously'— though he did not use those words. He spoke of behaving angrily without any feeling of anger inside, the mind being in control and untouched, so to speak.

I asked him about energy, à propos of something he said. Again he spoke exactly in accordance with Gurdjieff's teaching.

S.B. Every function needs its own quality of energy and that what is not needed for use for a function can be transformed into a higher quality for a higher function.

He also spoke about taking in energy through the breath, and said that what people can take in depends upon how they breathe and how they are inside. He recommended the practice of pausing after each inhalation and each exhalation about as long as it takes to draw breath (he said 3 to 6 seconds), and said that this greatly benefits the physical health, and that a man who trains himself to breathe that way should normally live to be at least a hundred years old. I said I had heard tell of monks living two hundred years and more. He said this was quite possible, and that with the aid of very special breathing practices, in which the air was held for a very long time, a man could even live for a thousand years. He said there was a close connection between the way of breathing and the length of life.

All the time, as he spoke, he was radiating this simplicity and goodness and love. At the same time, what he said carried exactly the same quality of certainty, of speaking not about theories, but about proven facts, which struck me so much when I first heard Ouspensky speak.

He spoke very interestingly of how one could learn by living with a guru, or teacher. He said that there was no question of teaching theory; it was completely practical. If one did something in the wrong way, the guru told one, 'This is the wrong way to act' —and in a few years one could learn to act in the right way.

As a last contribution to the picture of the saint's 'new light on old teachings', I shall quote what he said about impressions: that is all that enters our awareness whether from within or from without.

S.B. Our impressions out of the Infinite background are of three kinds, viz., sattwic, rajasic and tamasic: Advait, Viśiśthadvait and Dvait; soul, mind (or knowledge), and intellect (or activity). When we see a tree, there is its impression. Its existence alone is one impression. Its nature, like the idea that it begets fruits, it grows, its giving shelter, etc., also can be an impression. Again its usefulness, or the effect it produces, viz., that it is made into furniture, it serves as fire-wood etc., is also an impression. Thus we see that we can have an impression of a thing in three different ways. Advaits remain in the first kind of impression and speak, Viśiśthadvaits are in the second kind and Dvaits are in the third. We refer to these different impressions as Māyā and it is by stepping on one of these posts that we try to think of the Beyond. These three are the platforms from where Shankara, Ramanuja and Madhavacharya spoke of the Beyond.

Q. Why do we need the disciplines?

S.B. Because, when we try to mount on these platforms, we must beware of the misunderstanding. If we think "I am now able to see", we arouse our Ego-sense, *Ahamkāra*. This is like silt. It is like silt deposited by running water in a gutter. It comes with life naturally. To see the hidden surface of the gutter underneath, the silted mud should be removed daily. It is to neutralize the effect of this ego upon the true nature of our inner self that we are ordained to perform Yajna, Dāna and Tapas. It is owing to this ego, which is like the silt-coating, the true nature of our inner self is veiled. The effort on our part to remove this ego, which means to counteract its relation with our life, is Yajna, Dāna and Tapas. A piece of iron thrown in the weather outside naturally gets rusted. We should apply a certain wisdom to prevent this.

S.B. When we are able to look at the situation without interference from our ego-sense, then we can make sound judgments. The ego has no judgments of its own, but depends upon what it has seen and heard from others. That is why people dominated by their ego-sense, run from one school to another and believe everything that they hear. The foolish man accepts without testing for himself, and falls into confusion. This is what the three schools say:

Advaita—In the beginning man was perfect. He came down and took life in a fancy. And with life naturally he has his ego. This has kept him in the dark as to his own real nature. He should strive by way of Yajna, Dāna and Tapas and in the end he will get perfection again.

Viśiṣtadvaita—Man was imperfect in the beginning as he is at present. Through Yajna, Dāna and Tapas he will get perfection.

Dvaita—In His absolute state man was perfect but as he came down to the relative plane he became imperfect. In the end he again goes back to absolute perfection through Yajna, Dāna and Tapas.

S.B. But a wise man will not get himself involved in such controversial statements. He is concerned only with the state of complete freedom and happiness which is beyond this idea of perfection and imperfection. The common factor, that is this practice of Yajna, Dāna and Tapas, only will be counted by him rejecting all such speculative inquiries. He is right since these theories of perfection and imperfection are groundless. Because perfection in a relative plane can become imperfection in the absolute sense. For example. Our eyes are perfect as long as they maintain themselves but when compared to sight, that is their absolute sense, they are imperfect. Thus the same becomes perfect and imperfect also at one and the same time. All this the Shivapuri Baba observed, by saying that in perfection there is imperfection and in imperfection there is perfection. Neither of these separately can be called the Truth. Both together are the truth. By perfection, imperfection is understood and vice versa.

When we look from the ego-sense all is confusion. We see only contradictions and no hope of peace or even happiness.

S.B. We come out of the darkness (āvarana) and we go towards forms created by our own imagination (vikshepa). Beyond this darkness and these forms, lies the Truth that we are seeking. We must no longer dally with all this, but peep into the darkness (āvarana) which breaks our patience. Mind and intellect pull us towards this vikshepa side and we succumb. Therefore what we should do is to contribute always something or other to the soul side. For instance, in charity we spend more than what we spend for ourselves. This shows how we give more importance to soul instead of our life. In sleep, the exact time we keep in sleeping and rising from bed, shows our trend towards the soul. In meals etc., also, when we keep our principles fixed, we do contribute towards soul side. Likewise in every call of duties towards life, we can contribute always a certain amount for the benefit of our soul. This mind and intellect are just like a lighting switch which we turn off when we sleep. Whenever required we can turn the switch on again. So must be our attention towards life. Mind and intellect both together is what does the business of attending to our external life-demands. To turn off this switch when we have no duties and try to peep into the darkness is what we should do. There, we have neither mind nor intellect. Life is a wretched business. We know it. Mind and intellect tries to drag us down towards life. By leaving this vikshepa, or concrete experience of life, we try to peep into āvarana. A very painstaking business it is. We must penetrate into this smoky darkness. God may be in it or beyond it. So in Right Life, mind and intellect cannot play havoc. They are made use of only when required. At other times they are silent. They are caged like a lion and we shall not have to fear them. Promise or outside force makes us live the Right Life in the beginning.

S.B. We live on our impressions. The background is God. When we tread on the earth we are on the space occupied by our foot. When we change pace we change our resting place. Like this we have our impression of the different things we see in this universe. Where are we? Really we are on, we dwell within, the impression,

141

and when we change from one impression to another, we change our dwelling place. When we say—this is sun, and think of it, we are in this—our impression of the sun. We never keep alone. We go from one to another of such impressions. This means that we are not dwelling on the meditation of God, Who is the Absolute Background of all these various impressions. Now the question arises as to how we can free ourselves from such impressions.

S.B. We should know that these impressions are like pieces of understandings which rest on God, the Absolute Background behind. These are like parts only out of the Whole. We should here see that God, or the Absolute, is permeating each and every such impression of ours. We then penetrate into such impressions, and find that in essence all these pieces of impressions are One, not different. We find unity in diversity. In thus doing, we go from the vikshepa shakti of Māyā to the āvarana side. From there, we try to make out the underlying fundamental Unity. In thus contemplating, i.e. in the course of this inquiry, we drop off our impressions, which are varied, and remain in anxious suspense for the while. That is to say, we remain in vacancy having no picture formed in our mind. This state is to be compared to the state when we jump from a tree and in falling we are not yet touching the ground—only in mid air. Such is the moment when we get the vision of God.

CHAPTER SIX

THE REMOVAL OF DOUBTS

THE man who has seen God knows all and can do all. He can go no further for he has reached the Infinite. The question then arises whether he has any more duties. To this the Shivapuri Baba replied.

S.B. After God-Realization, the soul does not immediately leave the body. The Soul must stay on in the body so long as his 'prārabdha' enjoins it to stay. In the meantime the Soul should commune with the Absolute and, when the 'prārabdha' is finished, it will automatically go back to the Absolute. Any effort to shorten the process—that is, to end life earlier—would lead to another birth. The Soul must suffer the period ordained.

S.B. Since the body has to be maintained, the person who has attained realization has some duties to perform. His threefold duties having been ordered, disciplined and regulated, he gives to the world the knowledge and wisdom he has attained, and for his profession takes what is given by students and disciples. In this way he maintains his life.

S.B. Thus, one has to find the harmony between the Individual and the Absolute, and realize the Truth. Penance, yogavyas etc. deny life and, therefore, become blind to this harmony. By pursuing 'Right Life' and Meditation, this harmony is found and the deeper meaning of life is realized.

When we asked him the question whether his speaking with us was a necessary duty, he said that all three duties must be maintained until death. Speaking with people and removing their doubts was his professional duty. By performing it, he could receive gifts, and with them he could take care of himself and the family who looked after his needs. In that way all three duties were being performed. Moreover, he said, life must continue to be very exactly regulated. For that reason he would only see people and answer their questions at the fixed hours from ten in the morning until four in the afternoon. The remaining sixteen hours of each day were reserved for the care of the body and meditation.

The extremely precise regulation of the day's activities that he recommends raises a serious problem for those of us who live in the world—and the Western world at that. How are we to obtain the necessary tranquillity in the conditions of modern life? On this subject the Shivapuri Baba is, as usual, extremely practical. He says it is all possible through Right Living, without subjecting oneself to artificial conditions. He cites the Tantric schools of India with their elaborate austerities and devices for 'overcoming the world'.

S.B. Tantra says that the external world is quite against us, and so we should fight against it and achieve our object, i.e. God. This is the spirit of Tantra. Gita, on the other hand, advises us to put up with it simply according to time, place and circumstances. It leaves us to discriminate for ourselves, according as we are capable enough.

S.B. We have three proposals before us for coping with the problem of reconciling our life on earth with the search for God. One is Swadharma which says: "God in greater proportion and life very little." In Swadharma efficiency in life is not wanted and so ignored or, if cared for, very little only.

S.B. The second is given by the Laws of Religion, which in India establish the Varnāshrama-dharma—the four castes and the four stages of life. The rule here is: "God and life in equal proportion." In Varnāshrama-dharma—that is the rule of life by caste, custom and the ages of man—efficiency in life is given equal importance.

S.B. Then there are the various yogas which promise to show people short-cuts. There is Karma-yoga or dexterity in action, Jñana-yoga or the way of knowledge, and Bhakti-yoga or the way of devotion. All of these, according to the Shivapuri Baba, put "God very little and life to a greater proportion." In Karma, Jñana and Bhakti, efficiency in life is wanted totally first, and only afterwards God.

S.B. This does not mean that in the outward life we can be negligent or inefficient. Only the aim is not success, but strength of mind and serenity. The secret of this is to develop the power of keen observation so that we can in everything discriminate what is necessary and what is to be avoided. The following extract shows how he helped Manandhar to come to Swadharma.

S.B. We cannot but attend to the external life-demands. We all have our needs. For example, I needed to have my cotton chadar prepared. In every situation, we must attend to the necessary details. When you try to picture to yourself all the members of your house, you cannot see them all at a glance. Some of them may be missing. So in working out every situation we must bring Soul, Mind and Intellect with all the necessary details. Some of them may be missing.

S.B. Example! You undertook to frame the photo of Shiva Nataraj. Irresponsibility is shown. No prior plan in the light of the three principles and their details was made. The feeling of sacredness is lost sight of.

S.B. When we say 'Intellect', we must at one glance remember its various ingredients: that is the Indriyas and each of them with its eighty-four lakhs of varieties. In such stray works you must try to learn. This time it was a complete failure: no intelligence, no mind, no morality. Your knowledge, after having so many lectures, seems pretty enough, but it is only to look at. In reality, you are receding. What is known is not put into action.

Some early very practical counsels given to Manandhar show how the study of situations and the planning of action are to be conducted. Here are comments made upon a report on various successes and failures:

S.B. Failure to rise at the appointed time is not due to the influence of the gunas. Determination to get up at that time was there, which is beyond the gunas. Only it is because the habit is not yet formed to rise at the appointed time. It will be set right after a few days' practice.

If there is somebody to call on you, fix a suitable time to see him. Have a time fixed after meditation to see such people. Only if it is an urgent business we can have a break in our timetable and attend to it. If not, let it be only at the appointed time.

Before making a timetable we should be able to know what

abnormal situation may arise beforehand and make our routine accordingly. You have called the man to see you. So you know beforehand that he is expected. So also, your wife's being busy in going out for *puja* could be known beforehand and you could have made your routine accordingly.

Put up how much to smoke in the day and, even if I offer you cigarettes, you can desist from smoking more than what has been fixed.

Try to get established in Right Life before your leave expires.

Commission and omission is the defect of the mind. It is due to liking and disliking.

Determination is gunatita (above the gunas). If at all it is one of the gunas, it is sattwic.

About meals. Find out what is suitable for your body. Rice, dal and vegetables in reduced quantity is the ideal: but if it suits you, have one of the meals changed accordingly. No harm. One should have proper meals for right living.

Even more detailed instructions were given concerning the care of the body. He entitled his answer: *Shaucham*, meaning purity. *S.B.* Room should be neat and clean. It should be whitewashed every six months. Beddings must be dried in the sun every week or twice a month. Bed cover should be washed twice a week at least. Outer garments must be changed twice a week at least. For instance, a coat may be worn for two or three days, and kept to be cooled down for two or three days, and then can again be put on. Body heat will cool down by the time it is needed. As for the inner garments, we should wash them every day, so that the perspiration due to the body heat will not remain. The thing is one piece of cloth cannot be worn for more than twenty-four hours. If not, one cloth for this day, and, instead of washing it, we can keep it dry in the air, to cool down for another twenty-four hours, and then only can be put on. After coming back from latrine, we should wash our hands with soap or mud. After passing urine, hands should be washed with simple water. Bathe daily in the morning. Once a week, a special bath should be taken with soap in the sun. Hands should not touch any parts of the body at other times.

S.B. Like this we must engage our attention on the different actions for twenty-four hours. There is time and space which we must cover with such things though these are little things. Collectively they are very useful, in as much as we get fully occupied, and there is no gap anywhere between twenty-four hours. Gaps are like leakages, and, through them, we become victims to speculation, which is nothing but a waste of our energy.

It is not hard to see how this strict regime can be adapted to conditions of life in temperate or northern climates.

Another illustration, much later on, is taken from the incident of a drive in a car. I give the extract verbatim:

S.B. We had a drive. We enjoyed, but no! We suffered instead. This is the nature of life. We like pleasure and take to it, but, in the outcome, we take to pain. We know what dirt and dust we have now after the drive. In going to enjoy pleasure, an equal load of pain and suffering we had to bear all the time. The idea of pleasure that we enjoyed is but the creation of this mind, and we try to retain that pleasure at all costs. This is the world and its nature. We took to the idea and we get involved as long as the drive was not ended. We feel really happy only when we return to our original place. With the consciousness of our original place only we can take to it for the time being, because in that case we can come back to it again, or else we will be going after it always, and with it suffer all pains and troubles, mistaking them for pleasure. This world and its experience like this, is only the work of the mind. We create mind and then we have this world. Otherwise no world. Science has proved it. Originally, man's life is perfect, but not his 'I-ness'. After having innumerable pains and drawbacks, we become sensitive and then can silence the mind. For example, accidents like breaking of hands and legs, will keep the man away from such indulgings later on. Or driving the whole day without a break, the man becomes exhausted and he wants to do away with it.

S.B. The one crumbled and sent to the lowest bottom, the other allowed to rise to the highest above. In one, life is suffered most; and in the other, it is enjoyed most. Both sorts of people will never come back to this dungeon in the shape of this world. The right work of the Intelligence is threefold. It has to take stock of the content of the situation as it presents itself. We must see it as completely as is necessary, taking pains to be sure that no significant element is overlooked. Then we must discriminate in order to see what is relevant and what is irrelevant, what must be done and what is to be avoided. The third stage is to plan our action so that all unnecessary activity is eliminated. In the following extract there are several references to the Gita. Krishna plays a twofold role in the Gita. In one aspect he is the Maharishi, the Great Teacher—or rather the Source from which all gods and all teachers have come (Gita 10.2). In another aspect he is the Divine Principle within Arjuna himself: his *Purush-artha*. (Gita 8.4.)

The question turns upon the role of our power of attention, here called Consciousness. If its only true object is God, why do we have to turn it towards the World?

S.B. Right Life consists of three stages: (1) Simple observation, (2) Detection and (3) Elimination.

(1) This is the ABC of the business, the most painstaking part of it. If we get through it, the other two parts will be very easy. See what we do daily—Karma, vikarma or akarma. That is all. By doing this we retain our consciousness always with us, which is the most unavoidable preliminary for the other stages. At present our consciousness is like the light of a firefly (coming forth and ceasing). It should be retained eternally like the Sun's light, otherwise how can we work out our ideal (Right Life). This is very, very slippery at present, like the fish under water. By the continued practice of constant observing this consciousness can be caught hold of.

S.B. We should keep this consciousness always in our ideal or Right Life which is two-fold.

(1) The lower life, viz. the protection of life.

(2) The higher one, viz. the thought on God.

S.B. Some say that though they are not keeping their consciousness on God all the time, they are keeping this on the lower life. No, not exactly so. In their case their consciousness is outside both. It is immersed in life with interest of some sort. Consciousness should be made to act as our guide, and at the same time work with us in all our activities. Knowledge and energy, should go hand in hand.

S.B. Consciousness should remain aloof and guide our purushartha, that is the Gain of Merit, and at the same time work with us in doing purushartha. Compare Krishna as the guiding Consciousness and Arjuna as Purushartha. Krishna is there in Arjuna all the time in doing purushartha, and at the same time as the guiding principle aloof from him. *Karma phala tyaga*—abandoning the fruits of action—is there in this, when Consciousness guides us partly standing aloof; and, partly, working together with us. In the opposite case, it remains partly doing the work, and, partly, in the result accruing thereto. For example, with the help of a light we write something. If it is put out we cannot. Let this light be compared to our consciousness by the help of which we work. It throws light standing in its own place and, because by the help of the thrown light we work, it is as though working with us like one who is leading a blind man. What we achieve with this consciousness, in the above-stated two positions, is genuine and will never be lost but will enable the process to precipitate what is required.

He went on to illustrate his meaning by reference to a well-known story of the Mahabhārata, the burning of the Khandava forest.

S.B. Two lives were saved—one, the krouncha bird, another the Mayabin. The tapasya of Ugrabahu resulted in the life of the krouncha bird. Goodness done turns into reality or genuineness and it is never put an end to. Mayabin is the engineer of the Rakshasas which means that they are outside the real life. It stands for imagination which can build anything and everything, and it is required also for a man of right life. It enables him to work out his life according to his own Dharma and his life is thereby preserved. When Krishna and Arjuna come, the forest is burnt. So when consciousness and Purushartha work in right order all akarma and vikarma are eliminated. Only karma remains, which is again possible only with right or intention and with good imagination. We still require these two to keep karma going.

On another occasion:

S.B. All our thoughts and activities centre round our home.

Peace and happiness at home is our main concern. The preservation of our body and all its belongings has engaged our attention at present. We feel the necessity of preserving our life and hence is all this detail in the movement of our thoughts and impulses, which are so directed as to contribute in full measure to the well-being of our bodily existence. Thus we find that our body is the home round which our thoughts and activities revolve.

S.B. But as a result of our inquiry into the inner depths of our earthly existence, we find that our body is not ourselves. The finer principles beyond this body-consciousness which we call soul is our real self. This soul is to be known and realized for better identification.

S.B. This inquiry as to 'Who am I?' should be our main concern. This by successive stages will take us to our eternal truth or home where we shall find all peace and happiness. Freedom from ignorance and Bliss supreme will be the result.

S.B. So, to make this soul-inquiry possible, and thereby to attain the desired end, we have got to direct our attention in a proper way. Intelligence and morality have to be taken care of. Just as our life activities towards the fulfilment of our body preservation as aforesaid, this intelligence and morality will make possible our soul-inquiry. Our spiritual need is best preserved or fulfilled by our attending to proper morality and proper use of our intelligence, in the same way as our bodily need is well attended to by our life-activities as aforesaid. The problem of the soul is the centre round which our morality and intelligence revolve, exactly in the same manner as the problem of our body-preservation becomes the centre of all our activities at present.

In the earlier chapters, I have given several examples of practical advice connected with Swadharma. I shall now go on to show how he dealt with various kinds of questions put to him.

T. Manandhar: People ask me to explain, why ought strictness to be maintained in our life activities. How should I reply?

S.B. Truth is harsh and justice uncompromising. You should point out there is Siddhanta and there is Vedanta. Right performance of our duties, with all strictness and avoidance of non-duties (or commission and omission), is the Siddhanta or principles. Whereas Vedanta is for giving illumination in the principles, as to when we can deviate from the established principles of Siddhanta. That is, Vedanta speaks of some concessions at certain circumstances. There is no law that does not admit of fluctuation according to time, place and circumstances. It advocates some sort of discrimination in dealing with the established code or principles. If the deviation is actuated by one's desire or temptation, one cannot defend it with vedantic arguments, and likewise if it is actuated by fear. Temptation and Fear are the two causes for deviation which is wrong. Love of God (the idea that we can have the highest pleasure or bliss which surpasses every other sense-pleasure) saves us from temptation, and Distaste for life (the idea that death is inevitable and let death come in the attempt) brings fearlessness. Vairagya is love of God, plus the strength of tyaga. For instance, taking mushroom (which you took the previous day), if it is actuated by desire, it is wrong, because you succumb to temptation, but if it is taken simply because of accidents (that, too, only half the quantity according to rajas, and quarter according to sattwic, and full according to tamas), there is concession, because in this case we are not led away by temptation. Here comes Vedanta, but, according to Siddhanta, one must resist all temptation, and hence strictness has to be maintained. Siddhanta is Veda, and after Veda comes Vedanta.

S.B. The spirit of inquiry as to whence is this being is the main thing round which we should be centreing, when we are not performing our life-activities. That is Nirguna upasana. Saguna upasana is to be taken recourse to when mind gets disgusted and tired in Nirguna upasana, just for relaxation. Scientifically explained, it is like having the strong force of a guleli—a catapult—to throw the piece of stone. Saguna upasana is our playing with imagination, which is an aid in as much as it serves as a resting place for a traveller, who has to resume his journey again after a short relaxation. Imagining God in some way or other according to our preconceived notion is false. Yet it is to be sought simply to relax for some time and enter into God inquiry again with fresh vigour. Also, it is an aid like the mine-sweeper in the ocean which is laid with mines. It clears our onward way of all preconceived impressions in our mind, so that we can steer clear on our onward journey, that is, our inquiry.

S.B. Saguna upasana—Dhyāna and Dhāranā. We can meditate on any natural phenomenon like rivers, mountains, seas, etc., instead of a personal God, but not on artificial things.

S.B. Commission and omission—Their elimination and successful performance of duties makes life prosperous and easy. This has nothing to do with our soul-inquiry, yet when life is smooth-sailing we are not confronted with worries, and hence we can meditate without worries on the problem of life. To do an action successfully we need to learn the technique—Asuric sampad and influence of the gunas are to be avoided and subsequent experience will help.

Next comes a set of questions submitted in writing on such matters as the reality of the world, life after death, the transcendence and immanence of God. The comment dictated by the Shivapuri Baba runs as follows:

S.B. All the questions you have put are wise questions. From the very beginning of the world, inquisitive people like you have been discussing on these points and the discussions have continued up to this very day. But no two people have given the same answer. Every inquiry has ended in simple talk. Now if we also begin to speak on this we cannot come to a conclusion.

S.B. There is this world, and life should be possible here. For this possibility of life all those people have given us the same answer, that is, what I told you about the disciplines, and the answer for the questions you have asked you will know when you see God. The three disciplines which I had told you, if practised, will come to this. Now, these talked out matters you can know to a certain extent by referring to Yogavāsiṣtha and that Bhishma parva in the Mahābhārata. Now positively go through these two and then frame again questions.

S.B. Knowledge is twofold. One which deals with 'WHAT' and the other which is dealing with 'HOW', All the questions you have put come under this 'WHAT?' We can wait for this till we see God. But the question 'HOW?' should be solved today. We cannot wait till God comes. Hence be very strict and careful in this 'HOW?'.

This alone can reveal the other. Now, if you want to know my opinion on the questions you have put, I give a few in the following:

(1) Is life real?

S.B. This is a question you have put. Now whether this is real or unreal we cannot know. It is real in a relative sense because we are subjected to hunger, thirst and various other things which are practical. Now here we must do something to relieve ourselves. Hence the discipline I have told you.

(2) Is there life after death?

S.B. That is another question. Now when one goes to sleep he is dead, and again he gets up the next day, and again the life goes on as before. So after death also we come into life in another way. Therefore, there is no death but only life. Death is nothing but changing the old clothes for new ones, that is, from one body to another. Death is nothing but a sleep. Just as we sleep tonight and get up the next morning. We are what we were yesterday. So in future too we will be what we have been today. So build your life today and tomorrow you will have a good life. The present life— a poor living and a low status because, previously, we did not live it properly with right application of Morality, Knowledge and Intellect. How far we had moved ahead in the light of these principles, so far our present life is made. The man who has given a serious thought over this must get a chance to work along this line.

S.B. Morality is that which makes him capable to abide by this right Knowledge and right Intellect so to say, his spirit of self-surrender. Thought over God is equivalent to the thought over this Swadharma. When a man has given his word, or determined to live his life according to these principles of Swadharma, he is said to have lived it internally, though externally it takes sometime for him to live up to it.

(3) God is all in all and God is nowhere. How can it be?

S.B. Now you have employed a lot of people under you. You are the master of all. You give them clothes, meals, everything. That is, you are all in all for them, but in another sense you are nowhere.

Those people do their work and they gain their wages. In this sense God has created this universe and all of us. So he is all in all to us. But we must do our life-activities by ourselves and live our life. Here God is nowhere, and so on and on. I have answered only one or two questions here. For the rest you go through these two books: *Yogavāsiṣṭha* and the *Bhisma Parva*. Then you will have a speculative answer upon all those subjects you have inquired. I am particular only in these disciplines because this is of immediate value.

S.B. There is a story in the Puranas like this. A man was struck with an arrow. At once he was lamenting to take that arrow out of his body. He did not inquire where from that arrow came, whether it was steel or bamboo. His sole intention was to take it out and relieve his pain. When that was over he examined the arrow. He inquired about the shooter. Now, from this what we know is that the immediate thing is to release oneself from trouble and then to inquire. First if you inquire, the pain will be continuing and that is sheer foolishness.

S.B. So I ask you to practise the three disciplines and get yourself relieved from the immediate troubles. When you practise these disciplines, whatever difficulties and misunderstandings may come, questions should be framed and sent to me, to get them solved so that you can proceed.

I shall give now questions and answers exchanged with different people at different times. There is no systematic presentation of his teaching but rather the 'removal of doubt'.

Q. Why is there so much unhappiness in the world today?

S.B. This is not only today. The threefold miseries, or Tribidha Tap, are always with humanity. They are pain, worry and fear. When we live inside the kingdom of a king, we naturally have to pay some taxes and also to abide by the laws he has promulgated for the welfare of the country. If we refuse to pay the taxes, we will be denied his kind protection of our life and property, and if we do not live according to the law of the land, we will get punishment from him.

S.B. Just so we must think, is in the Kingdom of God. We must pay Him His dues or taxes; and, not only that, we must live according to the laws he has given us to abide by. What then are the taxes? Look, He has given us this physical body which we must protect. And whatever duties we have to perform daily for the maintenance of this body and its belongings are the taxes He has levied on us. This involves the protection of this body, our family, our relatives, and such other duties which have direct or indirect connection with our physical body. They are to be taken as Karma, and must be fulfilled without failure. Outside this, that is the actions which have no relation with the preservation of our physical body, we must know as a-karma and vi-karma. Thus by looking to our body-protection we pay the taxes required to The King and Emperor of the Universe. We will then be taken as right citizens by Him, deserving His care and protection. This sphere of activities is ruled over by our Intellect, because it is Intellect which plays the leading part. Our success depends upon a sharp intellect and dexterous action. Next in order comes our sub-servience to God's Law, which we call Morality. What is the Law and how can we be called moral? This part of the business in-volves our mind. It is always confronted with Ichchhā (Desire), Rāga (Attachment), and Dwesha (Hatred). If we keep our mind away from their influences we are said to be keeping up morality. Whenever we do our Karma we should do it without being im-pelled by desire, or by attachment, or by hatred. No liking or disliking we should have in doing our duties. In return for this we are exempted from any kind of punishment from God.

S.B. The first one, i.e. the tax-paying business, will ensure our physical welfare, while the second, i.e. this keeping up of morality, ensures our mental health and hence no worries. Again, if the rest of our time is spent in looking eagerly for God, we shall have no experience of Fear. Thus we prevent ourselves from falling into the three sufferings or 'Tribidha Tap' as it is called, and maintain our blissful state. We have only to keep our attention on these three channels and nothing more.

Q. You advise us to look only for Sattwic actions. What is Sattwic?
S.B. The wisdom with which a man sees the one fundamental unity in all creation, that is, by which he goes to the essence of things, is Sattwic. One who has got this equable frame of mind is

155

said to be of Sattwic temperament. A Sattwic action is doing one's fixed duties regularly without fail, strictly according to the law prescribed, with neither attachment nor hatred towards them, and without any desire or interest for the fruit of one's actions. A man without attachment to anything, without feeling any sort of pride in his work, with a steadfastness of purpose, and without being affected in the least by the resultant success or failure, is a Sattwic person. His is a clear insight, or right discrimination, of things and he has a resolute selfcontrol. Thus with a Sattwic temperament, a Sattwic wisdom and a Sattwic action combined, one should proceed with one's duties in life. Naturally such a man will cultivate and acquire both the commanding and the controlling power which is so very necessary. This business of living will become as easy as anything to him as he gets more and more used to it. He will then be a fully developed being capable enough to see life, Truth or God face to face.

Q. Why did a man like Ramakrishna not follow your three disciplines for Right Living. You say they are necessary for all: but the great saints like Ramakrishna and Ramana Maharshi did not live that way, did they?

S.B. That is because they had a very strong mind. For them, the first two disciplines were not necessary. For example Ramakrishna had only dilute Yajna, Dāna and Tapas—only for protection of life—only defensive side—all three done to extent not to lose life. Ordinary people do all three to gain and so they acquire an offensive character. The dilute one is quite sufficient for our purpose. In this the three purifications are also attended to, but only to the extent not to lose life. In Ramakrishna there is enough dexterity in taking to the temple-business and living with family so that he could manage protection of body. In Buddha too, enough dexterity was there in taking the food which came before him unasked. When the one thing is kept supreme, i.e. when God is aimed at at all costs, the three purifications come in automatically (though without a guru) to make the supreme one possible. Keen hankering after God drags in its train the required purifications even without our knowing to a certain extent, which is quite enough for our purpose.

Q. What is your attitude towards society. What social obligations should we fulfil?

S.B. One should perform the social obligations according to the prevailing social laws. If any law is found unsuitable, the individual may mobilize the opinion of the elders and may try to alter it. Manu Samhita was altered from time to time, and there are twelve Samhitas which testify to the fact that social laws are not permanent or immutable. But one should not try to bring disharmony to the society by personal whim. Those who want to change social laws must first make their lives on the basis of Right Life and then persuade others to see the defects in the social law.

S.B. One who has dedicated his life to the pursuit of TRUTH need not dissipate his energies on questions of social laws. Because his main task lies in the journey towards the Absolute, performance of social obligations becomes the least troublesome for him and, since he has not to follow any dogma or so-called religious exercises, he will personally not have to face any conflict with social questions.

Q. What is the position of women? Can they follow your Swadharma in the same way as men? Is there any fundamental difference?

S.B. Apart from the physiological and psychological distinctions there is no other fundamental distinction between man and woman. A woman like a man can also realize the Truth, if she follows the path of Right Life and Meditation. A woman has, however, some special duties to perform.

Q. You say that for Swadharma one must have a keen intelligence and a strong mind. Does this mean that it is only for people of a high order of spiritual development, for high souls, so to speak?

S.B. There is nothing high or low, great or small. Each individual can attain the highest goal in life, if he follows the Right Life and Meditation.

One must bring discipline in life—Mental, Intellectual and Moral Discipline. He should also use the discrimination, and learn to discriminate between right and wrong action, desirable and undesirable thing.

In personal life, one must be watchful of his own actions. He

157

should not perform a single unnecessary action. He should not see what is not wanted for him, should not hear what has no concern to him, should not speak what is not necessary, should not eat more than is required for the body, should not touch what is not needed. He should conserve all his senses and must not waste any of them. In personal life one must be pure in action and in mind.

Q. What is your view of modern science? Some people say that it has destroyed religion in the world. Do you believe that religion will be regenerated?

S.B. There should be no conflict between Science and Religion. They are complementary. Science has taken Religion to be its enemy which it should not. Practice of Right Life is a kind of science. There is no harm if science is able to bring any comfort to individuals and society. But science should not attempt to override Divine laws, nor should it be used to gain material wealth at the cost of social harmony.

Every religion is restricted by theories, arguments, blind faith, unnecessary and sometimes unwanted practices. Religion may at times create an atmosphere for good life, but it cannot fulfil the tasks ordained by God, nor can it by itself lead to God or Realization.

Meditation combined with Right Life can alone bring Realization. This method admits of no religion, no sect, no dogma, no theory. This is called Swadharma. In modern times, some Hindy Shastrakars have interpreted Swadharma as meaning holding on to *varnāshram* or caste theory. Swadharma simply means fulfilling one's own duties. Performance of three-fold duties and meditation is performance of Swadharma.

Q. What is the place of yogavyas in Right Living?

S.B. In search for the Truth yogavyas is not needed. Only the Right Life and Meditation will lead to Realization. Yogavyas may give some power, as knowledge of medicine or of engineering gives some power to men. Exercise of power attained by yogavyas is sinful and that creates more illusions.

I would pause here to draw the attention of the reader to this answer. When I spoke to the saint about the value of various powers acquired by spiritual development, he said: 'Powers, siddhis, will come, they are natural for man; but they are not to be sought after. If they come, they must not be used to gain power or for any other purpose except Right Living.' We were speaking of the knowledge of the contents of the mind of another. I said that a man who had attained God-Realization must be able, if he chose, to know what is in another man's mind and the state of his soul. He said: 'Yes he can, but to use this power would be sin. No one has the right to look into the mind of another.' This sound advice, which agrees so well with that given by all the greatest mystics, is sometimes forgotten, and we hear people speaking of 'powers' as a sign of spiritual development.

I have already mentioned the debt I owe to my good friend Tarzie Vittachi, who went ahead of us to Kathmandu to ascertain if the Shivapuri Baba were still alive and would see us. T.V. went again on his own account with an Indian friend, Bomon Behram, a well-known newspaper owner from Bombay. I shall reproduce his notes, which cover ground not mentioned in other talks.

The conversation began on the usual lines with a description of Swadharma.

S.B. Discriminating living is essential for a man's development. When we plan how much work, how much food and drink, how much time for professional work we should give, real living begins. We begin to think clearly because our minds become calmer, more disciplined. We begin to sift the true from the false and problems then already become less. All problems arise because our minds are linked to sentiment. We should link our minds to reason, not sentiment. Our mind will always follow what is pleasant, even if it is not reasonable. It will avoid the unpleasant, even if it is clearly more reasonable. Pleasure and displeasure, liking and disliking should not be the business of the mind.

S.B. We have to live in a country, so we must obey its laws. Otherwise there will be trouble. We have to live in our mind and body, so we must obey the law of our body and mind—which are the commandments. These are the disciplines given for ordinary man.

T.V. What proportion should be effort, how much surrender?

S.B. Take food, for instance. To eat only what your body needs is to surrender. To eat all you can is effort! Discipline is not effort but surrender. Discipline gives strength. A bird gets its strength from air. A king from his army. A man from his sense of discipline. Discipline gives a plan and shape to man's life. When he makes a start, already some problems become less. With each act of surrender, of discipline, it becomes easier to frustrate the mind's tricks to drag you away from your purpose. Like this:

S.B. A government official has his duties to perform for which he is paid a salary. But he takes a bribe and ruins himself. When you isolate your sense of discrimination, when you disobey the code which you say you value, it is like taking a bribe. For the sake of *extra* pleasure you ruin your life's possibilities. The Government official should learn to live within his salary—everything he wants must come from within that limitation. A man's life must be lived within a discipline—whatever pleasure he gets, he must get from within that limitation. Without discipline a man, be he a king or a Yogi, is but a human beast.

T.V. asked him about the upbringing of his children.

S.B. A child must be trained to be first, efficient, second, responsible, and third, aware of questions of why are we living, truth, God. Efficiency is very essential. Even making a cup of tea must be perfected by practice—trial and error. *Responsibility* must be learnt because this leads to concern for duty.

S.B. Concern for spiritual matters is needed because this *is* one's duty—to find Truth and God. Children should be given daily duties—a daily plan for life. Simplify their lives for them.

T.V. How?

S.B. By simplifying yours. It is possible to do your work and reduce the complexity of your life and theirs. They will imitate your life. It is more than mere imitation but even imitation will do for a start.

T.V. How should we organize our days' duties?

S.B. Spend some time *every day* thinking of why we are living? Where did we come from? Where are we bound? When a start is made this becomes interesting, like reading a book. When it is interesting other thoughts become weaker and one is thinking only of the book. Another analogy: Look for the white screen of the cinema behind the moving, flickering pictures. Cut activity down to the minimum and do our duties.

T.V. Have you any advice about food?

S.B. Take only half belly full of food, quarter belly of water and one quarter of belly empty.

T.V. What should be our attitude to pleasure and pain?

S.B. Our troubles arise because we have been taught to hanker after Happiness. This is nonsense. Māyā. The winter comes and the summer comes. We live through both. Pleasure and pain are like that. Life should not be spent seeking one and avoiding the other. Life must be lived according to one's duty.

T.V. But did not God give us so much abundance and pleasurable things also for our use?

S.B. They were given to keep us bound to the earth. Ordinary people want to remain bound to the earth. Some want to penetrate the darkness.

T.V. Is not this Earth our true home?

S.B. Our origins are far beyond space. We came from there and if we have followed our duty we return there.

T.V. Babaji says that what we call 'the good things of life' were given to enslave us. Why did God want to trap us?

S.B. There is no possibility of answer to that. When one has practised one's duty and eventually penetrated through, the answer becomes evident. It is possible to say something about this, now in terms of Karma, but it is not the truth. It is only a partial truth.

T.V. Babaji talks of enlightenment as though it is easier than it is normally made out to be.

S.B. But it is easier than it is normally made out to be. Do you imagine that Jesus, the Buddha and Mohammed and others would have asked us to follow commandments which only *they* could follow? Don't you see that it is profitable for certain people to make it seem more difficult than it is? It is possible to find enlightenment in the rest of your lifetime. Never mind yesterday, let yesterday be forgotten. Begin today. Now. That is the only way. This world is a painful place. What is the use of pleasure if it is replaced by pain? This is a very dangerous world. We must find Truth in the time left to us.

The End of an Epoch

T.V. Does the world grow and degenerate periodically? Why do people build and destroy what they build—even civilizations?

S.B. Everything we build must be discharged and rebuilt. This is a periodical process. Every 100 years some change takes place. Every 1,000 years some great change. Every 2,000 years the end of an epoch. Every 6,000 years a major disaster to civilization. Every 12,000 years a complete change. We are now at the end of a 6,000 year cycle.

T.V. Will the destruction you foresee be localized?

S.B. No. It will be everywhere. In cities and villages. Something will be left behind to carry on this world with people who have sensed and seen the results of material living.

T.V. How does one prepare for this? Not escape this—but prepare for this?

S.B. There is only one way. Begin to do your duty now. And meditate on the meaning of one's life.

T.V. Pak Subuh said that disaster would break out 'like mistake'.

S.B. Yes. It will appear like a mistake.

T.V. What is man's place in the universe?

S.B. In this solar system there is 'human' life only on this Earth. But there is something similar on planets in other solar systems. The beings on Jupiter are of a different structure from ours. A realized soul with 'Bodhi' goes right back to the origin which is beyond space. Others to other planets—'heavens and hells'—or may return to this earth—'purgatory'.

T.V. and B.B. then asked questions about Subud and the Great Life Force. He said that this in Hinduism is called Shakti.

B.B. Is Shakti what we achieve by spiritual practice and meditation?

S.B. Shakti is our own power. We are its Master.

B.B. Who is Me? What is me?

S.B. 'I'. The 'I'. I must be master of Shakti.

T.V. I have experienced in the Subud latihan the feeling of a

162

force within me that makes me conscious of various things that are happening in, around and to me. I make movements, speak, sing, laugh or cry, but I am conscious of these actions and can stop them when I wish.

S.B. Therefore 'I' is conscious. 'I' is in control of 'Shakti', this force. In this latihan, you enjoy the experience of this force, do you not?

T.V. Yes.

S.B. This is wrong. This is not the aim. The pleasure it gives, the fine liberated feeling it gives is not the purpose. The purpose is to find the truth. This force, this Shakti which has been awakened in you is to help you to find Truth.

This force is not God. It was created, therefore it is not the Creator. It is like this. The king issues money to give you power to do services for him. His image is on the money and has power. But it is not the king. It is what he has created.

This latihan of Subud is a very good practice for you. It will calm the mind and give you enough strength to enable you to follow the ultimate teaching which is to do one's duties. For a Buddhist the five Silas to develop character, the eightfold path to discipline the body, and meditation to penetrate through to the ultimate truth. Subud can take you very far—to pure consciousness and therefore enable you to find the truth for yourself. But do not neglect the main teaching—the commandments and contemplation. This must go hand in hand with your Subud latihan.

In Subud you have experienced happiness through latihan. Don't dwell on this. This is not the purpose. It blocks your development, your possibility of deeper understanding. Suppose you do not achieve this happiness in latihan? Will you not be anxious that you have not experienced something? This anxiety is more valuable than the happiness. It is like this: a child dies; the mother is unconsolable and cannot be distracted or diverted by any offer of pleasure. We should be like this mother because we have not yet achieved 'Bodhi'.

B.B. Is it necessary to give up everything like the Sannyasins to discover the truth?

S.B. No. Sannyasins are in complete revolt. Grihasthas (house-

163

holders) are in complete slavery. Both are degenerate. Why give up life? Accept life. Why leave life? Live it. But it is necessary to live it dutifully, responsibly.

T.V. How to begin right living?

S.B. Go back to your book. Never mind what it is. You are a Buddhist. Read and reread the Sermon on the Mount. It contains the essence of Buddhism.

This most interesting talk demonstrates the advantage of being bold with one's questions. Those I shall report next came from a group of friends in England who had no idea what they could dare to ask. The questions and his answers were recorded on tape and after transcribed by one of the ladies present. At least, therefore, we have the advantage here of hearing his own words and manner of speaking. I read out the questions as follows:

J.G.B. May I put to you some questions sent by a group of friends in England. The first is from an old gentleman Mr. K. He asks: 'What value has art compared with charity? Through beautiful things, such as music and painting, we feel ourselves drawn towards God. Is art, then, something valuable for man, or what position does it occupy in our lives?'

S.B. One is never drawn towards God by art and music: we are drawn to beauty only. Yes. One is never drawn towards God.

J.G.B. Art lifts up the soul. Is that not towards God?

S.B. No. It will only give you the excellent beauty of God— not God Himself.

J.G.B. But beauty comes from God also, does it not?

S.B. But now you see it from a distance (he holds out the rose he is holding in his hand). This is beautiful. Can you have the smell?

J.G.B. Not from here.

S.B. The Beauty of God you can know through art and music. But God you cannot know.

J.G.B. Does not beauty draw us up towards God?

S.B. But God is still a great distance away.

J.G.B. Would you say then, Babaji, that from the point of view of coming to the knowledge of God, art is no longer valuable for man?

To appreciate the emphatic answer it would be necessary to

hear the vibrations of the word 'harmful' as he pronounced it. It gave an impression of scornful warning not to underestimate the danger of being led astray by the love of beauty.

S.B. Not only not valuable—harmful also! Mind will not empty of all its contents. Yes! The more beautiful, the further away from God. Yes! Ugliness and beauty: both must vanish from the mind.

M.V.H. But, is there not some art which seems much higher than others, like the Sphinx, the Taj Mahal, or the Elephanta Caves with the great Trimurti. That art seems to appeal to another side of us.

S.B. But at that time when you see them, you forget yourself, you forget God! Then that beauty alone prevails in you. The essential things are forgotten. Individuality is forgotten. God is forgotten. That beauty only prevails in you at that time. What is the advantage here? I will tell you. Every trouble of the world is gone. One is very happy here. That is all. The unhappiness of this world is not felt.

J.G.B. But sometimes it is the opposite. There are some religious subjects—they are very common in Christian Art, and also some music, such as the Gregorian Chants for the Passion, that bring us into a vivid sense of the suffering of the world. There is no forgetting unhappiness here.

S.B. No. It is only beauty. There may actually be a relationship and yet it is only beauty that prevails in the mind.

J.G.B. We must reflect on what you have said. I can see that it is important to distinguish beauty as a manifested form and God Who is beyond form. Obviously, we must not be captivated by form to the exclusion of what is beyond.

I have another question from a lady Miss W. Her difficulty is to understand the right balance between concern with one's own personal salvation and concern with the suffering and needs of the world. She wants to come to the knowledge of God, but she also feels the duty of service in the world. The world is suffering, it has many needs that arouse our compassion. What should we do?

S.B. Let those needs wait. First go to God. When one sees God, then one can take to these things. Remember: 'First seek to enter the Kingdom of God and everything can be added towards that.'

For the present, if one cannot help oneself what help can one give to another? That is it.

Suppose, however, you still want to do some help. Here in these duties, there is a chance. In one's obligatory duty towards home and society, one can give a little bit—according to one's capacity.

J.G.B. One must not try to go beyond the limits of one's obligatory duties?

S.B. Yes, that is all. If you want to do good for the whole of humanity, wait until the knowledge and the power come.

J.G.B. My next question comes from a lady who recently lost her husband. They were very united and she feels herself lost without him. She feels that she must know what happens after death for without that knowledge she cannot have peace.

S.B. Death is like sleep. We do not know what will come when we awaken. Before seeing God, it is not possible to know. Yes.

J.G.B. But if one has not peace of mind, meditation becomes impossible. You yourself, Babaji, have impressed that on us.

S.B. Peace of mind is not there because the virtues are not there. When the virtues will come, there will be peace of mind.

J.G.B. Can we say then: from moral discipline comes the purification of the mind, from this come the virtues and, with them, peace of mind; from peace of mind comes the power to meditate and from this we come to the knowledge of God. Then all these questions are answered.

S.B. It is so. Yes.

J.G.B. The next comes from a young man J.B. He says: 'I have heard about the three duties and I can see that they are right and proper for man. Then you come to moral discipline and say that this means to be free from like and dislike. This is just what I cannot do. When I try to be free from dislike of someone, nothing happens. I still dislike them and I am not free. I know I must be free from it. But I don't know how to start. Can the Shivapuri Baba show me how I can set about it?

S.B. First of all, you must see that like and dislike is a defect in man. You must recognize it as a defect and never justify it. You must understand that unless it is removed, one cannot see God. This understanding must come.

J.G.B. Do you mean that we must see it as an obstacle on our path, and that it comes from our lower nature that is drawing us away from God. So long as we are subject to liking and disliking, especially of people, we shall never come to our goal? Do you say that by this understanding alone liking and disliking will diminish.

S.B. Yes. He must be patient and persevere. It will come.

J.G.B. The next question is about Faith. She says: 'Meditation must come before we can see God, but you tell us that meditation is based upon faith. But how can we have this Faith? From where does this faith come?'

S.B. Because I am existing, you are existing, the world is existing. Wherefrom all these things came? From this existence, one should have faith. Yes. No other way. There is this existence. What is this? There should be something behind this.

J.G.B. If we have a question, there must be answer. Is that what you mean?

S.B. It is so.

J.G.B. So, if we are able to ask the question: Why do I exist? there must be an answer to it. So there must be some reason why I exist. If I believe that—which I must believe or I could not even ask the question—then it follows that I believe that there is a Source from which it comes. So I have faith. So I understand you rightly?

S.B. Yes. There is this thing we see. (He holds out the rose in his hand). We must have faith that there is a rose flower in the world. We see! Now, to prove your existence, what proof can be given? Because I see you—that is the proof. No other proof is possible. This very existence: what is this? There is a Creator of all these things. Or if you cannot see that—then you must say: 'There is a Truth beyond this existence.' One must believe that. From this the rest will follow.

J.G.B. Mrs. D. S. asks about prayer. She prays for help—sometimes for herself, sometimes for someone else who is in trouble. Sometimes help comes in a wonderful way and she feels sure her prayer has been answered. Sometimes help does not come.

'If we sincerely ask for help', she says, 'perhaps for some other person without any egoistic reason, and it does not come, is this because we did not have enough faith? Or because one asks from the wrong place in oneself? Or perhaps help did come and we were just blind and could not see it?'

S.B. Because it is from wrong place. Or it may be wrong persons or wrong event. One of these reasons. Yes.

J.G.B. We ask in the wrong situation?

S.B. In the wrong situation. Yes. Either the persons may be wrong or the event may be wrong.

J.G.B. Mrs. A.T. asks how it is that man—especially the Western man of today—has come to be so dominated by his thinking that his mind has become weak. The strong mind you say is needed for meditation simply is not there, it is weakened by too much mental activity. How did we get into this situation?

S.B. It is because of man's own habits. Suppose your habit is to eat more. Disease automatically comes. Now remove that habit of eating more. That disease will go. If one is more engaged in life it becomes a habit. Extra love is given for life. Extra prominence is given to life. That means the intelligence must work for life and the mind is neglected. That is the way it happens.

J.G.B. If we did not give so much importance to our external activity, there would not be so much exaggeration of thinking?

S.B. Yes. There is more liking. The proportion is more for life and less for moral discipline. In that way, the mind cannot go towards God.

J.G.B. This leads on to the next question from Mr. H. S. He heard from me about the three disciplines and was most favourably impressed with the simplicity and objectivity of your programme of Right Living. But, he adds: 'You know what are the conditions of Western life at the present time. There are so many pressures of life and activity. Everyone is busy all the time. Is there any way that you would recommend for Western people in their conditions of life, by which they can specially follow your disciplines?'

S.B. The conditions of life are very much the same for all. He should take to the disciplines. He can use his Intelligence to plan and perform his duties. He will have more time for meditation. He should devote himself to the virtues. That will strengthen his mind. These disciplines in themselves will give him a chance.

J.G.B. But peace of mind is necessary. They have more peace of mind in a village than in the city.

S.B. But there is also pressure—even in the village.

J.G.B. In the forest, then?

S.B. You see. Mind is always filled up with various thoughts and other things. Empty the mind—even in the busiest life—one is free. Yes, mind is crowded.

J.G.B. Does this mean that the fulfilment of the three disciplines is the same for people of all natures and all conditions of life? For example, in a family there may be two brothers of the same parents, brought up in the same conditions, receiving the same education, and yet, their spiritual natures can be very different. I take it that the two brothers should not follow the same way: one is right for one, and another for the second?

S.B. Yes. That is the nature of the world.

J.G.B. But it is also one's own nature. What can be done if we do not know our own nature.

S.B. Yes. One's own nature one must know. You must study, and understand and then improve, that very nature.

J.G.B. We have a question from Mrs. M. K. about natures. 'If when we were in childhood', she says, 'we did not develop the moral disciplines, afterwards it will be very difficult to come to meditation.'

S.B. The parents have that responsibility. They have to teach their children discrimination. Then they will come easily to the three disciplines.

J.G.B. You told my wife about this. But if discrimination has not been taught in childhood, does it mean that there is little hope?

S.B. Still it is possible. When you know it today, try to practise it from today. It is possible.

J.G.B. Is it then never too late? If one has the desire to come to God, it is still not too late?

S.B. Not too late.

J.G.B. The two remaining questions come from two young scientists, who say that young people everywhere are very distressed about the present state of the world. They do not know what will be the future towards which they are going. For what have they to prepare themselves?

S.B. Prepare for today. That is all. Prepare for today.

J.G.B. But what of the future? Some young people ask if it is worth preparing anything if the world is going to be an impossible place to live in.

S.B. When the future comes, according to that we can adjust. The world will never be the same for today and tomorrow. Totally different! There is no steady world. Every minute there is a change. Today your body is like that: prepare a part for that like this. The proportions the body needs will have changed tomorrow. Then you can see.

J.G.B. You told us that great changes are to be expected.

S.B. It is so. A big revolution is to come now. This civilization is spent up. It cannot give happiness to people. It will be removed.

M.V.H. How can we prepare for these changes? Or can we only prepare for the day?

S.B. It is beyond our capacity. We can enter into these three disciplines—that will help. No more help we can get.

This ended the conversation—which I have reproduced in full except for one or two very personal questions to which he gave the appropriate answers.

On the last occasion we visited him I told him that the lecture I had given about him and his teaching had aroused great interest, and many people wanted to know about the three disciplines and bring them into their lives. He seemed pleased and said that if any of these people had doubts and difficulties, I was to write to him and he would reply.

I took the opportunity of asking him whether he approved of working in groups. I was quite prepared to do my best to transmit his teaching if a few people came together and asked me to do so. The following conversation ensued:

S.B. Yes. It is good for people to come together. They can easily understand my teaching, because it has no complications. You must explain the duties. For the moral discipline, they can read the sixteenth chapter of the Gita. Then they can come together.

Each of them will produce his doubt. Many will begin to answer. Many will come to know. The association of such people will be very nice. Yes. Always half-an-hour, or an hour's discussion on our own life, among these associates it helps.

J.G.B. Quite a number of people have asked me to tell them about your teaching. Some are serious. But I take it that if they only ask out of curiosity, it is not worth it.

S.B. No. Not worth. One should begin to *live* this life. This jijñasu, one who wants to know only, but does not wish to live; for him it is not necessary to explain. For those who want to live and want to have Reality, for them only this is good.

J.G.B. And the other thing that really comes up here—this way to enter into this life of discipline and meditation—this requires already qualifications; so that it seems that what you tell us comes at the end of ordinary teaching. It presupposes a clear understanding of what one desires to achieve.

S.B. It is so. The only qualification essential for this is the desire for God. That is the only qualification.

J.G.B. You mean, if there is that desire, there will also be the readiness to accept discipline?

S.B. Yes.

J.G.B. But supposing that a man has desire for God, but has formed many bad habits so that his mind is always disturbed, can he already begin to follow this way from his desire, or should he first practice discipline?

S.B. Simultaneously. For one who is qualified, he can live with the minimum for life; but for such a man he should add some more enjoyable things to it, and then slowly reducing. So extra things for enjoyment. Those who are not qualified for this, they have got many bad habits in life. They have got a desire to enjoy also. For those people, these three duties, plus some choice duties also for their enjoyment. Slowly these choice duties must vanish, and these three duties must remain.

J.G.B. I did not understand what you meant. Did you say, *choice duties*?

S.B. Yes. Now, he is not satisfied with these three duties, he wants an extra enjoyment. So long as that strong desire for that extra enjoyment remains, for that particular enjoyment, he can choose some choice duty.

The Shivapuri Baba had pointed to the tape recorder on which I was registering our conversation and said:

S.B. This is a choice duty.

He went on to explain that in addition to the three obligatory duties and the four charities, there are activities that are not harmful and therefore do not count as vikarma. A man may undertake such an activity because it interests him. When he does so, he must do it as well and as faithfully as the obligatory duties. It becomes a part of his outward life which must be done 'without commission or omission'.

Nevertheless, the choice duties are to be regarded as a concession to the weakness of our minds. They are not necessary for our lives and as we become more attached to God and less to life, we shall let these choice duties diminish and finally drop away entirely.

J.G.B. If a man has a very great love for music, and then is not able to free himself from his love for music, well, then he can study music in a special way just to satisfy this desire, until he is ready to let it go.

S.B. Yes, practising for some day; when the desire for God increases, that can be let go.

In subsequent letters, dictated to Manandhar, he amplified the principle of choice duties. This principle permits an orderly transition from the customary conditions of life to those which will be present when the love of God has come to dominate over all other interests in life.

The Shivapuri Baba's doctrine is of great importance for our present time, although for most people it would represent a psychological revolution they could scarcely contemplate. We undertake all kinds of activities believing them to be profitable, interesting and even objectively good for humanity or at least our immediate society. We become involved in this work believing that it really matters—that it is 'pleasing in the sight of God'. We have no means of knowing whether this is true or not, unless it is commanded by the religion to which we give our assent. But what religion commands proves on closer examination to be comprised within the three disciplines. We are commanded to do our duty, to act morally, to perform the four charities and, beyond and above all, to love and worship God. All religions agree upon these disciplines. They have very little else to command or require of man.

If we stop to ask ourselves under what category come many of our most cherished activities, we shall be forced to admit that not so many come under the head of obligatory duties. It is already something if we can call them 'choice duties'. Only too often we drift into activities, and afterwards call them obligations, because we are either too proud or too timid to admit that we do not know why we are engaged in them at all. It is salutary; whenever we are considering the undertaking of some new activity we should ask ourselves whether it is an obligatory duty of one of the three kinds, or whether it is a 'choice duty' that we undertake because we want to, or whether it comes under the heading of useless (akarmic) or even harmful (vikarmic) activity. When we are able to say that we are doing something because we want to do it and choose to do it, then we are being honest about it, and not pretending to ourselves or others that it is for the sake of humanity or the love of God. This will help us to keep our choice duties in their right place, and, above all, not to become slaves of our own activity. If we can submit ourselves to this discipline, we shall come near to the requirements of Karma Yoga to perform actions without concern with the fruits. (*c.f.* Gita 6.1. *Anāśritah karmaphalam kāryam karma karoti*).

This reference to the Gita reminds me to compare the Shivapuri Baba's advice with that given to Arjuna by Krishna, which forms the exposition of Karmayoga in Chapter 3 of the Gita. Krishna points out the obvious fact that we cannot exist and not act. (3.5). Nor does non-action lead to perfection (3.4), because anything that exists owes a debt to help in maintaining the world (3.16). Thus action is both unavoidable and obligatory.

The mistake is often made of confusing unconcern with fruits with unconcern with action itself. The Shivapuri Baba saw the dangers of this confusion which can lead to a kind of quietism in which life itself is regarded as a burden to be shed. No justification for this view can be found in the Gita and the Shivapuri Baba was at pains to emphasize that all the elements of Right Life are valid and necessary. Simple enjoyment of bodily pleasures is a form of God-Realization and only ceases to be so if we cling to enjoyment or desire it to the point of forgetting that it cannot be maintained without the moral and spiritual disciplines. The Gita in Chapter X shows how we are to look for God in everything. 'In the vital forces, I am the life, in the material world, I am the treasure, in fire, earth, sky, heaven, sun, moon and planets I am the characteristic energy and among mountains I am Meru, the Axis of the World.'

This attitude is to be taken seriously and not regarded merely as a transient phase that will be left behind. Within this attitude are comprised all legitimate activities of man that go beyond the limitations of the obligatory duties. Life can and should be lived to the full in all its departments: but in this full living we must never lose sight of our goal which is God. For this we must learn to look for God in every action. There is God in the discipline of duty that leads to Self-Realization, there is God in moral discipline that leads to Soul-Realization, and there is God in spiritual discipline that leads directly to God Himself. Beyond all these is Liberation, Moksha, but this does not mean that life ceases to be lived until the chosen moment of release has come. All the duties and activities of life are to be performed, with the one essential condition that we must never take them as the final goal. If we identify ourselves with them, we lose the point of our existence — which is to come to the Knowledge of God, or if we prefer it, to Objective Truth. When we do, we shall still perform actions, perhaps more indefatigably than before, but we shall do so because it will have become objectively necessary for the preservation of the world order. If we are not foolish enough to suppose that we have attained Objective Truth, we shall be content to describe our activities for the 'good of mankind' as choice duties. They will serve as a bridge over which we can pass from ignorance to wisdom. This does not mean abandoning life but living it wisely, that is according to the three-fold principle of the complete life. As the Shivapuri Baba says, this complete life is both prior to all religion and common to all religion, and to any satisfying account of the reason for our existence upon the earth.

We are, however, too easily inclined to think that we have chosen the way of perfection when we have not even begun to see what it will cost. I will end this book by recording our last talk with him, before we took our final farewell to his earthly form.

The conversation came out of the perplexity of the ladies who were with me to account for the strange behaviour often to be observed in people who assert that their sole longing is for the spiritual life.

M.H. I think that so many people say—I have heard them say it—they want God, and really they have no conception that God is much further away than we think. It is rather what we have talked about. It is a sort of 'spiritual immaturity'.

S.B. They do not know the magnitude of the trouble.

J.G.B. That is it.

M.H. And it is very difficult. Because people will say 'All I want is God', but realize they are in a sort of dream.

S.B. When they are asked to follow this discipline—

M.H. They would not do it.

S.B. When they do not come to discipline, they should be rejected. They are not for it. If one really wants God, he will willingly take to this discipline. If one will not take to this discipline, then he is lukewarm only.

J.G.B. By means of various spiritual exercises people do have experiences, and they also feel that they are being liberated from the pressure of the lower forces; they feel themselves less angry, for example, and they are less attracted by money and for pleasures. So they say, I am nearer to God, but perhaps it is only something that is happening in their nature. It is not really spiritual yet.

S.B. But still if they have got such virtues with them, they are in a sense nearer to God.

J.G.B. Only it is a danger always for us to make the mistake of thinking that we are nearer the end than we really are.

S.B. It is so. It is so.

J.G.B. Because I think probably that the man who really comes near to God, really comes to the point where he has no more hope, and he thinks, I will never find God, but, if I die, I will go on looking. Then it is possible, as in your story. If this boy had thought that perhaps in three lives he would do it, he would have been afraid of the lion; but, as he had to live many thousand lives, he did not fear the lion.

S.B. That King Yudishthira tells Krishna he wants God. Then Krishna was saying: Those who want Me, I will give him all sorts of troubles in this world. If he will not mind these troubles, then I will give him all sorts of pleasures in this world. If he ignores these pleasures, then only will he have Me. Yudishthira—you see to what troubles he was subjected. He was driven out of his kingdom, he had to lose even his wife, various troubles came, but he never cared about them. Then he was made the Emperor of the World, every pleasure was given to him, but he did not accept all those pleasures. Then only he could get to God.

M.H. And Job, our patriarch, too, in the Bible, went through all these terrible sufferings and destructive things, and yet, he said, always he had faith in God.

S.B. Yes. That is it. Everything goes against us, till we know God.

J.G.B. Some, who have practised seriously the method of deep meditation for several years, say that they come to a point where a plunge is made into the darkness. The consciousness becomes clear but empty of all forms. In this state, they not only feel bliss, and peace, but also the confidence that God were somewhere present. They want to know if this is the right direction.

S.B. The final is God-Realization. This may be on the way, seeing such things. It may be hallucinations, or it may be some truth of their Guru's teaching; but this is not the final.

J.G.B. This experience of bliss and peace and confidence, is not the final end?

S.B. No.

J.G.B. Is there anything else that should be said?

S.B. The sum and substance of my teaching is this: live the minimum life possible, subjecting body and mind to strict discipline. Again, how a very hungry man longs for meat, how a man suffering from intense cold longs for heat, so long for God, meditate on Him continuously. And this is the sum and substance of my teaching. That is for you, that is for them, that is for the whole world. It is by this that I saw the Truth, and I am happy. Yes.

GLOSSARY OF SANSKRIT WORDS

Adrishta

Unseen, unforeseen. Hence the invisible power or destiny by which existence is moved. In man, this power is his supra-consciousness of which his ordinary self is unaware.   121

Advaita

Non-dualism. This takes the form of asserting that there is only one ultimate Reality which is Brahman or the Supreme Spirit—all else is illusion. Also spelt Advaitabad.   78, 88, 117–20, 139–40

Ahamkāra

Literally means 'I am the doer'. In classical Sanskrit literature, this is taken in a pejorative sense to imply egoism and arrogance. It can also be the sense of self, the 'I-feeling' present in us, by which we relate ourselves to objects. Hence the S.B. says 'Ahamkāra ascertains'.   100–1, 107, 126, 139

Akarma

Useless activity or actions. These fetter the mind and make meditation difficult or impossible.   97–8, 127, 134, 148, 155

Ānanda

Bliss which comprises the three states of Sukha, Santosh and Shānti (*qqvv*) which result from performance of the three disciplines: bodily, moral, and spiritual.   122

Anāsakti Yoga

The rejection of powers and enjoyments in order to attain God-Realization.   121

Anaśrita karmaphalam kāryam Karma karoti

Not caring for the fruits of action necessary actions are to be performed.   173

Artha

Wealth or possessions. Can be used also for spiritual or psychic gifts. The second of the aims of existence.   61, 79

Atman

The breath of life and hence the soul. In philosophy, the True Self. Commonly used to mean simply the nature or character of a person. Atmatattwa means the essential nature of the self on which S.B. says man should meditate.   117

Āvarana

Covered and concealed: guarded from sight, in philosophy: the obscuring power of Māyā.   141–2

Bhakta

Originally meant the dividing of food for sacrifice. The man who gives a part of his possessions becomes a worshipper or devotee. Hence Bhakta came to signify the man of devotion. Bhakti is devotion.   120, 132

Bhāvanā

Coming into being or causing to arise. Hence a notion, supposition or way of understanding. A good bhāvanā is the right attitude to every problem.   101

Bhrams
Illusory or wrong understanding.

Bhūta
The stem bhū is one of the fundamental sounds of the Indo-European languages. It means 'being-through-becoming' i.e. dynamic as distinct from static existence. S.B. takes it as anything that has come into existence, especially living creatures such as animals. 125–6

Bodha
In ordinary language, it means understanding, intelligence or wisdom. It is used by the S.B. to designate the state of God-Realization. 41, 136–7, 162–3

Citta
From stem cit: to perceive and also to care about. Citta commonly means attention and purpose and hence the mind or heart. It is used in philosophy to designate the condition of fluctuating consciousness. The S.B. treats it as the instrumental awareness which shows us how to act. 122, 126

Dāna
From stem Dā to give or to restore. Liberality, generosity. It is of four kinds cf. p. 94. 58, 93–4, 120, 139–40, 156

Dhāranā
From stem dhā: set in a direction and hence to fix the mind. Dhāranā is a state of intentional and purposeful recollectedness. Generally, dhāranā is performed with the help of an image or object. It includes the use of mantras (q.v.) 110–15, 134, 152

Dharma
From the stem DHR: to sustain and to withstand, to use and to possess. In its common meaning Dharma is the law from which it comes to mean the Divine Law identified with Prajapati the Lord of Creatures and of Procreation. Dharma is also Yama the Lord of Death hence its significance as the Law of Existence in time rather than of Essence in Eternity. It is the first aim of existence. 52–8, 60, 77–80

Dhyāna
Dhyā: to direct one's attention and so to reflect or meditate upon a definite theme. Dhyāna is meditation by the creation of a mental image. 110–13, 134, 152

Dvaita
Dualism in all of its many forms asserts that there are two realities, God and the World or the Individual Soul and the Supreme Being. The dualism of India is not so much that of mind and matter as of the infinite and the finite. Also spelt Dvaitabad. 76, 88, 117–20, 139–40

Dwesha
Conveys the notion of division into two opposites. Hence aversion, dislike and even hatred. The man dominated by tamoguna is moved from passivity only by the pressure of unpleasant experiences. 105, 125, 135, 155

Ichchhā
Wish or desire. When used as a suffix it implies an intentional or voluntary action. The S.B. says that life according to Sattwaguna is characterized by Ichchhā which must mean that it is based on intention rather than passion or illusion. Vide Raga and Dwesha. 105, 135, 155

Indriya
Originally meant that which pertains to Indra the Saviour God of the Vedic hymns. Hence Indra's chief quality of saving strength. Later meant virility and finally all the organs of sense, the five indriyas are the five senses. 123–6, 136, 145

Jiwa

From jiv: to live. It is the principle of life, the living and personal soul of
man. Jwanmūkta means that state of having attained liberation while still
living on earth. The jiwa as personal self is not to be confused with the
purusha or individual self.   54, 85, 97, 109

Jñana

Primarily means knowledge attained by perception and investigation i.e.
scientific knowledge. In Yoga it is given the special meaning of detachment
from all objects of attention other than God alone and hence Jñana comes
to mean the path of enlightenment through the intellect.   120, 132

Kāma

Desires and their satisfaction. In ordinary use, K. refers to sexual passion.
In philosophy, K. is the third primitive aim of existence.   61

Karma Kaushala

Means dexterity that attains the result without arousing opposition.
Cf. Mahābharata.   100

Karma Phala Tyaga

Abandoning the fruits of action.   133, 149

Kshetra

Primarily a dwelling-place. A field or plot of ground. Figuratively the
womb and hence a wife. It is also the dwelling-place of the soul, i.e. the
physical body. Cosmically, it is the universal receptacle or ground of
experience. It is the field of self-realization of the Jiwa (q.v.).   71, 76, 122

Kshetrajña

One who knows fields and places, and hence the Purusha (q.v.) the 'dweller
within' the soul. C.f. Kshetra which can also be understood as the feminine
counterpart of the Kshetrajña.   71, 76

Lilas

Play, sport, grace, beauty and hence also spontaneity. Specially referred
to Vishnu in his Krishna appearance, whose manifestations are characterized
by grace and exuberance.   41

Manas

The internal organ which integrates sense perception and cognitive perception.
Usually translated as mind; but also sometimes a soul, heart, intellect, desire,
and disposition. It is certainly more than the power of cognition. The S.B.
uses it with the implications of desire and disposition e.g. a 'strong mind'.
                                                        84, 95, 100, 122, 126

Mantra

Prayers or hymns recited by priests. Later used for any kind of charm or
spell and also for wise sayings or counsels. In the practice of yoga, mantras
in the form of words or invocations are used to steady the mind in dhāranā
(q.v.).   111-12

Marga

The way. Thus Jnānamarga is the way of knowledge, Bhaktimarga: the way
of devotion, etc.   132

Māyā

The Supernatural or magical power by which illusion is created. Hence, the
world of illusion and unreality. A magician is said to exercise his 'Māyā' when
he makes his audience believe in his illusions. In Vedānta philosophy,
the illusion by reason of which one takes the unreal universe to be really
existent and as distinct from Supreme Spirit.   60, 90, 101, 120-1, 130

Moksha

Deliverance from bondage. In philosophy, it means the final liberation. This is the fourth aim of existence that goes beyond existence itself. 60, 61, 174

Nirvikalpa Samādhi

One who attains to this stage enjoys bliss in an undifferentiated state of consciousness. This is not true God-Realization. The man who obtains NS is liable to fall into self-deception. 90, 109, 114–15, 133–5

Niyama

Voluntary self-restraint; i.e., the performance of non-obligatory duties (v. Yama). 40

Pitri

Properly Pitr, father. Also 'the Fathers' in their ever-present spiritual reality. The Manes. Ancestor-worship is pitriyajna; but the S.B. gives it a different meaning as the acts we perform for the benefit of our ancestors such as sacrifice and acts of piety. 93–4

Prakriti

The primary state of matter. Undifferentiated hyle. That which is the support of the phenomenal world. 19, 117, 122–4

Prārabdha

Means literally that which one has undertaken and must therefore complete. Used to signify the potential for existence inherent in the individual soul which must be used up before the soul can return to the Absolute Source that is beyond Existence. 143

Purusha

Primarily a male human being. In philosophy it designates the common life-giving principle in man and in the universe. It is opposed to *prakriti* which is the physical body as part of the material universe. Purusha is commonly taken to mean the indwelling spiritual self.

Purushartha is the merit acquired by the self through right action; as Arjuna is required to do by entering the battle. It is commonly used to mean achievement in life. 71, 76, 78, 85, 96–7, 101, 113, 120–4, 136

Rāga

Primarily colour and especially redness. Since this colour is associated with sexual attraction, Rāga means charm and loveliness. The man dominated by rajoguna is swayed by what attracts and repels him. His satisfaction is in the fulfilment of his desires which he pursues with relentless activity.
105, 125, 135, 155

Rishi

From the stem rsh which conveys the notion of a smooth flow. Hence the ancient bards who transmitted the sacred hymns and teachings. And so poet, saint, sage or teacher. Rishiyajna is the offering to the Rishis and so Vedic prayers. Now taken to include spiritual study, holy association and service to one's own teacher. 93–4

Sādhanā

From sadha: to lead straight, to accomplish an aim. 130

Sādhanā is the general term for any kind of exercise or practice for the attainment of an aim. It is usually applied to the spiritual exercise of yoga; but Christian prayer is also called Sādhanā. A Sādhu is one who lives a virtuous, excellent life. 29, 31

Saguna

Having attributes or qualities; the opposite of nirguna: the undifferentiated state. 77, 151–2

Samadhi

Literally putting two things together. In religion it stands for the state of union of subject and object from which all sense of separateness is banished. In modern usage various types and stages of S. are recognized. In philosophy there are only two types, Savikalpas and Nirvikalpas.   109–10, 113–16, 121–2

Saṁsāra

The word Sāra means a way or track. Hence, Samsāra is wandering from place to place. From this it came to signify life in general and especially the 'wheel of existence' in which individual souls return again and again to various forms of embodiment.   86, 99, 129, 131

Santosh

Serenity or contentment with what one has. Regarded as a very high moral attribute.   98, 108, 122, 132

Sat

Neuter form of Sant which means that which really exists. The feminine Sati is used for the self-immolated widow who has attained imperishable reality by her sacrifice. Sat means the real world, that which is self-subsistent. *Cf.* Ch. Up. 'In the Beginning: Sat'. In philosophy, Sat is one of the three attributes of God, the other two being Chit and Ārarda.   122

Shakti

Ability and power. The three attributes of kingship. The attributes of a divine being and especially Shiva. The power of a word or syllable. Hence all kinds of gifts that have the quality of imagination and fancy: e.g. the poetic gift. In Tantrism the feminine aspect of Shiva.   142, 162–3

Shānti

Peace that comes from liberation from craving for existence.   60, 98, 109, 122, 123

Shāstra

Instruction, precept or rule: but especially the sacred writings from antiquity, *i.e.* the Vedas. In modern usage, various branches of learning are recognized such as Mānava Dharma S. (social laws), Jyotisha S. (astronomy) etc.   88, 131

Shoucham

Pure and stainless. Also lacking in nothing. Trusted and found to be without fault.   146

Shravana

The act of hearing. That which is received or announced by the power of hearing.   104

Siddhi

Originally the success of the archer in hitting his target. It has come to stand for the magical or supernatural powers ascribed to yogis and saints (sadhus). The operation is practical and external: i.e., the achievement of an overt aim. The siddhis include healing of mental and bodily sickness, prophecy, divination, levitation. the power to produce an illusory body that can visit remote places and to produce changes in matter. Siddha = endowed with Siddhi.   123, 130, 159

Sukha

Literally, ease, an easy, pleasant and comfortable life. A state of pleasure, primarily as regards outward circumstances.   60, 87, 98, 108, 122, 127, 132

Swadharma

Literally: one's own dharma (*q.v.*) S.B. uses it to mean right living in the sense of the best possible use of our time on earth.
      8, 13, 40, 60–1, 75, 77–9, 88, 94, 114, 120–1, 127–8, 131, 143, 153, 158

Tapas
Primarily heat. From the notion of heat of fermentation comes the derivative meaning of austerity and penance. Tapas may be physical or mental. S.B. takes it to mean 'lawful activity'. 93, 94, 120, 139–40, 156

Tattwa
Literally 'the state of being that', hence the essential native of anything. Tattwa-jnana is knowledge of the world as it really is, i.e., beyond its illusory appearances. It is relative knowledge as opposed to absolute knowledge. 40, 122–7

Tribidha Tap
The three-sourced suffering that is inseparable from the state of embodied existence. They are pain, anxiety and fear. 154–5

Turiya
The fourth transcendental state of consciousness in which the Purusha is free from illusions of Maya. It is contrasted with the other three states: *viz.* waking, dreaming and dreamless sleep. 90

Vikarma
Actions that are harmful to others and incur retributive consequences.
97–8, 127, 134, 148, 155

Vikshepa
Literally that which is thrown about and scattered. It has acquired the significance of projected image, and hence the diversifying power of Māyā as distinguished from the obscuring power of Māyā. 141–2

Viśiṡthadvaita
Uncompromising non-dualism (see adwaita) which asserts that the individual soul and the Supreme Spirit are one and the same and that this is the only Reality. 88, 117–20, 139–40

Yajna
From the stem yaj: worship by sacrificial offering. It now includes all forms of devoted service, c.f. Brahma y. Rishi y. Pitri y. Bhuta y. and Manushya y. These are described on pp. 93–4. 93–4, 120, 139–48, 156

Yama
From *yam* to hold and sustain. It means self-control in the performance of our obligatory duties. 40

Yoġavyas
or correctly Yogā Bhyāsa from Yoga and abhyas which means activity and practice. Yogavyas means to exercise oneself in one of the forms of Yoga.
88, 111, 143, 158

INDEX

The day before he died